Eyes of Compassion

EYES OF COMPASSION

Learning from
Thich Nhat Hanh

Jim Forest

~

ORBIS BOOKS
Maryknoll, New York 10545

Library of Congress Cataloging-in-Publication Data

Names: Forest, Jim (James H.) author.
Title: Eyes of compassion : learning from Thich Nhat Hanh / Jim Forest.
Description: Maryknoll : Orbis Books, 2021. | Summary: "A personal portrait of the life and teachings of Vietnamese Zen master Thich Nhat Hanh" — Provided by publisher.
Identifiers: LCCN 2020046364 (print) | LCCN 2020046365 (ebook) | ISBN 9781626984240 (trade paperback) | ISBN 9781608338870 (epub)
Subjects: LCSH: Nhất Hạnh, Thích. | Nhất Hạnh, Thích—Teachings. | Buddhist monks—Vietnam—Biography. | Compassion—Religious aspects—Buddhism. | Religious life—Zen Buddhism. | Buddhism—Doctrines.
Classification: LCC BQ9800.T5392 N45745 2021 (print) | LCC BQ9800.T5392 (ebook) | DDC 294.3/927092 [B]—dc23
LC record available at https://lccn.loc.gov/2020046364
LC ebook record available at https://lccn.loc.gov/2020046365

There is no boundary
between the sacred and the profane.
– Thich Nhat Hanh

for Nancy,
my collaborator in just about everything

Contents

Contents

Introduction

In a few days, it will be the Mid-Autumn Moon Festival, *Tet Trung Thu* in Vietnamese. I will take a leisurely walk beneath the full moon and pause at the crest of a hill. I will lift my face and sing a song I composed thirty years ago while celebrating Tet Trung Thu with my children at Plum Village, the meditation community founded by Thich Nhat Hanh:

> *Quiet, so quiet*
> *Quiet as a flower breathes*
> *I bow to the smiling moon*
> *the light in my heart*
> *She reflects in the fragile wings*
> *of the chanting insects in the fields*
> *creating vast strands of pearls*
> *ten thousand tiny moons*
> *Cast your seeds like precious pearls*
> *beneath her fragrant light,*
> *Seeds of sorrow soon transform*
> *into shining seeds of joy*

After my walk, I will sit on my deck with a small pot of tea and slices of mooncake, and celebrate not only this *Trung Thu* but the anniversary of the day, forty-seven years ago, when I first met Thich Nhat Hanh. Jim Forest played an essential role that made that encounter possible, and I will lift a cup of tea toward the moon, grateful for the inspiration Jim provided in 1972 to a nineteen-year-old classics student and peace activist in Austin, Texas.

I arrived in Paris on a brisk September day in 1973 and found my way by Metro to the southern suburb of Sceaux. I located boulevard Desgranges on a map and lugged my suitcase down its length until I arrived at the apartment building that housed the living and work quarters of the Vietnamese Buddhist Peace Delegation. I was about to meet Thich Nhat Hanh (Thay) and Cao Ngoc Phuong (later ordained as the Buddhist nun Sister Chan Khong) who had invited me to join their community as a full-time volunteer. Standing in front of their apartment door, I sensed that my life was about to be shaped in profound and lasting ways.

That I was standing there at all was due to in large part to Jim Forest. I had just turned twenty and in the past year had withdrawn from studies at the University of Texas at Austin in order to devote myself full time to the peace movement. Despite the signing of the Paris Peace Accords in January 1973, the war in Vietnam was still raging, still orchestrated by American policy and presence, and I had felt called to respond. I had been deeply touched by Jim's *Only the Rice Loves You*, published in the fall of 1972, that described spending a month with Thich Nhat Hanh and Cao Ngoc Phuong and other members of the Vietnamese Buddhist Peace Delegation.

Reading Jim's words came on the heels of my discovering a copy of Thich Nhat Hanh's *Lotus in a Sea of Fire* in a used bookstore. Published in 1967, it was an uncompromising call for peace that also offered a window onto Vietnamese history and culture. When I saw that the foreword had been written by Thomas Merton, I experienced a sudden sense of recognition and connection. In my late teens I was equally drawn to Buddhist and Christian contemplative traditions. I sat *zazen* on my own and read Christian mystics. As I increasingly felt called to an activist response to the war, I questioned how to integrate a contemplative practice with an activist life. Discovering that two monks from different traditions, Zen and Trappist, considered each other brothers and were fully engaged in peace work that was rooted in their lives of prayer and meditation was an affirmation. I longed to find a way to best engage my own heart and hands.

Jim's *Only the Rice Loves You* set my feet on a path I would walk for the next several years. Inspired by his words, I wrote letters to Thay and Chi Phuong in France, and also to Laura Hassler at the Fellowship of Reconciliation in Nyack, New York, to ask how I might support the peace, reconciliation, and reconstruction efforts of the Vietnamese Buddhists. Laura, described in *Only the Rice Loves You*, had recently returned to the United States after living as a volunteer with the Vietnamese Buddhist Peace Delegation. She had set up a liaison office to assist their efforts and encouraged me to come to Nyack and join her.

With a few essential belongings in a backpack, I travelled to Nyack. Once there, I was offered a rent-free room, basically a walk-in closet, by a pacifist couple. I was delighted and thought of it as a monk's cell. I set up a small altar on which I placed my Greek New Testament and the hardened cookie of a laughing Buddha, a Chinatown gift from Jim, who also lent me a cassette player and his collection of Thomas Merton's talks to novices at the Abbey of Gethsemani.

That summer was filled with liaison work, vigils in New York, fasts for peace, and nonviolent civil disobedience at the White House—and also deepening friendships with Jim, Laura, and other peacemakers.

At the end of the summer, an invitation came from Thay and Chi Phuong to come work with them in France. With Laura's departure, they had a need for someone who could assist with English-language correspondence.

So there, in mid-September 1973, I stood before their door. Feeling a bit nervous, I breathed, then knocked. The door opened a crack and then wider to reveal a smiling Chi Phuong. "Why didn't you call so I could pick you up at the train station?" she scolded, and then ushered me in. Within minutes, she was asking me to help translate a letter written in French into English. It was then that Thay entered the room. Slow, quiet footsteps. A quick exchange of words with Chi Phuong. "He says I will frighten you away by putting you to work so soon!" I protested that I was there to do work, but Thay insisted that we first brew and enjoy a pot of tea.

Work wrapped up earlier than usual that day. Thay explained it was the day of the Mid-Autumn Moon Festival—Tet Trung Thu. Chi Phuong described how Tet Trung Thu was celebrated in Vietnam with lantern making, children's processions, singing, and moon-gazing. Friends arrived that evening bearing platters of fruit and moon-shaped cakes filled with sweetened mung bean paste. Tea was served in delicate cups. Singing and storytelling ensued, as well as gazing out the window at the radiant moon. Thay asked Anh Huong, a scientist friend who was also a poet, to translate the story of Cuoi into French for me about a poor woodcutter who floated to the moon on an enchanted banyan tree.

It was a magical beginning to my years with the Vietnamese Buddhist Peace Delegation, marked by elements that soon grew familiar because they were woven into daily life: singing folksongs, writing and reciting poems, shaping and wrapping sticky rice into traditional cakes, brewing pots of tea, telling jokes. Amidst urgent and pressing work, receiving visitors, planning and preparing speaking tours and benefit concerts, all in response to the unrelenting devastation of the war, Thay always made room for moments of happiness. Thay's insistence on being happy in the present moment is, I think, his most radical and transformative teaching. Rooted by mindful breathing, it is the key to healing trauma past and present, ancestral and contemporary.

Many of the recollections and anecdotes that Jim shares in this memoir are familiar to me, as I was either present at conversations or had similar encounters with Thay's teaching. Those were rare years, darkened by the war's ongoing devastation, and yet also blessed by a certain smallness. Thay had not yet become internationally renowned as a Zen teacher. He was, in fact, reluctant to even teach Buddhist practice to Westerners, expressing the thought that people might better benefit by renewing their own ancestral traditions. Yet delegation members, Vietnamese as well as French and American volunteers, were always reminded to practice mindfulness. The breath, Thay pointed out, is available to everyone from any tradition.

Mindfulness served as the warp and weft of our days. Watching Thay scrape the sauce from a plate or wrap a New Year cake, pour a cup of tea, hoe a garden row, or dip a brush in ink for calligraphy—every act was lovingly performed; every act became a ritual. In Sceaux, we did walking meditation down an alley that Thay dubbed "Dog Shit

Lane" because only mindful steps could avoid the many unscooped dog turds. One August, to celebrate my birthday, Thay insisted Chi Phuong drive us in the delegation's tin can car, a brown *Deux Chevaux*, to the Champs Élysées. We did walking meditation on that grand, brightly lit boulevard and then stopped in a Belgian café for *pommes frites*. Thay knew I had gone to high school in Brussels and thought I might be nostalgic for Belgian cuisine. Always, such simple acts of kindness!

Some of my most enduring memories of that time are when Jim Forest and his family came for visits. There was always thoughtful, serious discussion. But there was also playful teasing, and after we moved to Fontvannes, walks in fields of sunflowers and plucking ears of baby corn in a neighboring farmer's field to make sweet soup. And singing, always singing. Laura had a voice like rain, Thay remarked, and Mobi a voice like a waterfall. Thay was especially fond of Jim's rendition of a folksong about a lumberjack who stirred his coffee with his thumb. Chi Phuong sang Thay's poems he had set to music in a voice that stilled and captivated us.

I learned to speak and read Vietnamese at Thay's side as he guided me sentence by sentence through books he had written. It was a privilege and joy to translate his books. But Jim did something I did not and for which I am forever grateful. Jim journaled. Jim sketched. Jim took photos. Jim was rarely without a journal or camera. I sometimes wondered if he was missing out on the experience of the present moment because of it. I was wrong. This memoir shows how awake Jim was to all the moments he spent with Thay. It also reflects Jim's profound generosity. Thanks to his journaling, sketching, and photographing, many moments continue to live and can be savored by a wider audience.

Thanks to Jim's devotion to recording his friendship and experiences with Thich Nhat Hanh, we are offered a unique portrait of Thay's humanity—his love of children, his sense of humor, his boundless compassion.

So on Tet Trung Thu, I will raise a cup of tea to Thay, to Jim, to the Moon that is the light in our hearts, that all beings might transform seeds of sorrow into shining seeds of joy.

Mobi Warren
September 2020

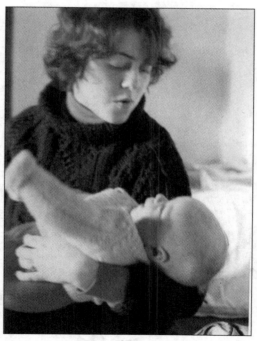

Mobi Warren holding my son Daniel at the apartment in Sceaux

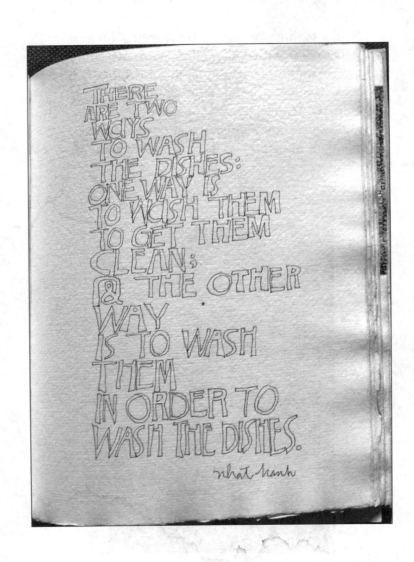

THERE
ARE TWO
WAYS
TO WASH
THE DISHES:
ONE WAY IS
TO WASH THEM
TO GET THEM
CLEAN;
& THE OTHER
WAY
IS TO WASH
THEM
IN ORDER TO
WASH THE DISHES.

nhat hanh

Washing dishes

I was in a cramped apartment in the outskirts of Paris in the early 1970s crowded with Vietnamese refugees plus one or two English-speaking guests. At the heart of the community was the poet and Zen master Thich Nhat Hanh, whose name at that time wasn't widely known. An animated discussion was going on in the main room just out of earshot, but I had been given the task that evening of doing the washing up. The pots, pans, and rice bowls seemed to reach half way to the ceiling in that closet-sized kitchen. I felt really annoyed. Stuck with an infinity of dirty dishes, I was missing the main event.

Somehow Nhat Hanh picked up on my irritation. Suddenly he was standing next to me. "Jim," he asked, "why are you washing the dishes?" I knew I was suddenly facing one of those very tricky Zen questions. Saying it was my turn wasn't adequate. I tried to think of a good Zen answer, but all I could come up with was, "You should wash the dishes to get them clean." "No," said Nhat Hanh. "You should wash the dishes to wash the dishes." I've been mulling over that answer ever since—more than four decades of mulling. I'm still in the dark. But what he said next was instantly helpful: "You should wash each dish as if it were the baby Jesus." That sentence was a flash of lightning.

While I still mostly wash the dishes to get them clean, every now and then I find I am, just for a passing moment, "washing the baby Jesus." I have recovered the awareness that sacred space includes the kitchen sink. And when that happens, though I haven't left the kitchen, it's something like reaching the Mount of the Beatitudes after a very long walk, in part thanks to the guidance of a Buddhist monk from Vietnam.

One action

I first met Thich Nhat Hanh in May 1966.

At the time Lyndon Johnson was America's president. The steadily rising level of U.S. troops in Vietnam reached 384,300 that year and within the next eighteen months would expand to half a million. But support for the war was shrinking. The nation had become deeply divided— never before had so many Americans opposed a war being fought by their own government. There were huge protest demonstrations in many cities. Conscientious objection was on the rise; thousands were refusing to serve in the military. Young men were burning their draft cards or crossing the border to Canada.

A significant part of the war's opposition was religious. In America the ranks of protesters included many prominent Christians and Jews, while in Vietnam tens of

Vietnamese villagers hiding in a canal

thousands of Buddhists, many of them monks whose monasteries had been scarred by war, were engaged in antiwar activities. Display of the Buddhist flag had been banned. In 1963, one leading Buddhist monk, Thich Quang Duc, had stunned the world when he burned himself alive in response to anti-Buddhist repression by the U.S.-backed Saigon government.

In July 1965, Al Hassler, executive secretary of the Fellowship of Reconciliation,[1] had led a fact-finding mission to Vietnam that included meetings in Saigon with Buddhist leaders who had organized demonstrations that had been brutally attacked by South Vietnamese police. The monk who most impressed Hassler was the Zen master Thich Nhat Hanh. A friendship quickly took root between them that was to influence the rest of both men's lives. Hassler wanted Nhat Hanh's voice to be heard in America.

Alfred Hassler and Thich Nhat Hanh together in Saigon in 1965

When I met Thich Nhat Hanh at the Fellowship of Reconciliation headquarters in Nyack, New York, he was thirty-nine and I was twenty-four. I had just been appointed director of the Fellowship's Vietnam program while also serving as co-secretary of the Catholic Peace Fellowship.

In introducing him to the FOR staff, Al Hassler explained that Nhat Hanh was the leading figure in the development of "engaged Buddhism," a movement of religious renewal that linked insights gained from Buddhist teaching to hands-on engagement in situations of suffering. He was a founder of Van Hanh University in Saigon and had played a leading role in efforts to bring the several strands of Vietnamese Buddhism into greater harmony, resulting in the creation of the Unified Buddhist Church. He was also the initiator of the School of Youth for Social Service, which prepared hundreds of young Vietnamese volunteers to serve in war-torn rural communities. In Vietnam he was a widely read author, though almost unknown outside his homeland. None of his twelve volumes of poetry or other writings had yet been published in English or other Western languages.

This was not Nhat Hanh's first visit to the United States, Hassler added. For nearly three years he had studied comparative religion at Princeton and lectured on Buddhism at Columbia University. His current U.S. visit had been made possible by an invitation to speak at Cornell University.

Thich Nhat Hanh in 1966.
Publicity photo by Al Hassler used by the
Fellowship of Reconciliation

Addressing the Fellowship staff, Nhat Hanh described the impact of the war on ordinary Vietnamese people, the obliteration of entire villages, and the actions of the Buddhist-led peace movement that allied itself with neither side. His stress was not on politics but on war-caused suffering. "The fact that the war kills far more innocent peasants than it does Vietcong is a tragic reality of life in the Vietnamese countryside," Nhat Hanh said. "Those who escape death by bombings are forced to abandon their destroyed villages and seek shelter in refugee camps where life is even more miserable than it was in the villages. In general these people do not blame the Vietcong for their plight. It is the men in the planes who drop death and destruction from the skies who appear to them to be their enemies. How can they see it otherwise?"

I was impressed not only by what Nhat Hanh had to say about his homeland but by his entire manner. He was as modest as the dark brown monastic robe he was wearing. When questions were raised, he looked at whomever he was addressing with alert, unhurried, attentive eyes. He spoke slowly, carefully, sparingly in Vietnamese-flavored English. His quiet voice reminded me of wind bells. There were restful silences between words and phrases. Afterward I said to Al Hassler, "I could listen to this guy for hours even if he were reading aloud from a telephone book." Al laughed. "Me too!"

I don't recall Nhat Hanh speaking of "mindfulness" that day, a word with which his name, five decades later, would become firmly grafted, nor did it occur to me that his teaching would circle the world, important not only to his fellow Buddhists but to many Christians and Jews, plus people who attached no religious labels to themselves.

It certainly didn't cross my mind that he would become a widely read author whose books would sell in the millions of copies. At the time, I saw him not as a religious teacher but as a peace advocate. But I left the meeting deeply impressed, aware that this humble monk from Vietnam was the sort of person who changes lives.

At the end of his informal talk, Nhat Hanh recited one of his poems:

> *Listen to this:*
> *Yesterday the Vietcong came through my village.*
> *Because of this my village was bombed—completely*
> *   destroyed.*
> *Every soul was killed.*
> *When I come back to the village now, the day after,*
> *There is nothing to see but clouds of dust and the river,*
> *   still flowing.*
> *The pagoda has neither roof nor altar,*
> *Only the foundations of houses are left.*
> *The bamboo thickets have been burned away.*
>
> *Here in the presence of the undisturbed stars,*
> *In the invisible presence of all the people still alive on*
> *   earth,*
> *Let me raise my voice to denounce this filthy war,*
> *The murder of brothers by brothers!*
> *I have a question: Who pushed us into this killing of one*
> *   another?*
>
> *Whoever is listening, be my witness!*
> *I cannot accept this war,*
> *I never could, I never shall.*
> *I must say this a thousand times before I am killed.*

I feel I am like that bird which dies for the sake of its mate
Dripping blood from its broken beak, and crying out:
Beware! Turn around to face your real enemies –
Ambition, violence, hatred, greed.

Men cannot be our enemies–even men called "Vietcong"!
If we kill men, what brothers will we have left?
With whom shall we live then?

In the question period, I asked Nhat Hanh if a monk's self-immolation is approved of in Buddhist tradition. "While the world press speaks of it as suicide," he responded, "in essence it is not. What Thich Quang Duc was aiming at when he burned himself three years ago was to move the hearts of the oppressors and call the attention of the world to the suffering being endured by the Vietnamese people, most of whom are Buddhists. To burn oneself is to prove that what one is saying is of the utmost importance. By burning himself, the monk is saying with all his strength that he can endure the greatest suffering in order to protect his people. To express his will by self-immolation is not to commit an act of despair or destruction—but to perform an act of construction—to suffer and to die for the sake of one's people. This is not suicide."

I also asked him about his name. "I was born with a different name, Nguyen Xuan Bao," he responded. "Your family name comes first. 'Nguyen' is my family name and 'Xuan Bao' the name I was given at birth, but when you are ordained as a monk you receive a new name. 'Thich' is the Vietnamese form of the Sanskrit family name of the Buddha. All Vietnamese monks are 'Thich.' My personal name, given to me when I was ordained, is 'Nhat Hanh.' It means 'one action.'"

Thich Quang Duc's self-immolation

Afterward, he asked me about the Catholic Peace Fellowship, adding that "in Vietnam few Catholics are peace workers." We were, I explained, a group affiliated with the Fellowship of Reconciliation. Our main work was assisting young Catholics who, refusing to take part in war, were seeking recognition as conscientious objectors. We were counseling hundreds of people every month. In addition we were also organizing what we called "Meals of Reconciliation." These were simple dinners, often held in church basements, in which participants shared rice and tea plus a few examples of Vietnamese cookery while hearing readings from Vietnamese literature—in fact mainly translations of poems written by Nhat Hanh—and listening to speakers who has witnessed first hand the destruction the war was causing. We hoped participants might leave these meals in a state of deeper connection with Vietnam that would strengthen their antiwar commitment. The

Fellowship of Reconciliation was now greatly expanding the Meals of Reconciliation project, making it ecumenical and interreligious.

"We need a Catholic Peace Fellowship in the Catholic Church of Vietnam," Nhat Hanh commented.

Brother against brother

Thanks to their conversations in Saigon in 1965, Al Hassler had realized that Thich Nhat Hanh had the potential to help pro-war Americans, including legislators, rethink their Cold-War perceptions about what was happening in Vietnam. Nhat Hanh's first public appearance was on the first of June 1966—a press conference in Washington at which he presented a Vietnamese Buddhist proposal for ending the war.

Nhat Hanh prefaced the plan with the reassurance that he was not anti-American. "It is precisely because I have a great respect and admiration for America that I have undertaken this long voyage to your country, a voyage that entails great personal risk for me upon my return to South Vietnam. Yet I assume this risk willingly because I have faith that if the American public can begin to understand something of what the Vietnamese people feel about what is happening in our country, much of the unnecessary tragedy and misery being endured by both our peoples might be eliminated. . . . If anti-Americanism seems to be emerging as a focus for some of the recent protests, it is because the Vietnamese people recognize that it is really only the awesome U.S. power that enables the Saigon government to rule without a popular mandate and to follow policies contrary to the aspirations of the Vietnamese people. This is not the independence for which the Vietnamese people fought so valiantly [against France's colonial ambitions until the French defeat in 1954]. The war in Vietnam today pits brother against brother, the Vietcong against the supporters of the Saigon government. Both sides claim to represent the Vietnamese people, but in reality, neither side does."[2]

Thich Nhat Hanh's five-point peace proposal called for the United States to make a clear statement of its desire to help the Vietnamese people to have a government truly responsive to Vietnamese aspirations; end the bombing in both North and South Vietnam; limit all military operations by U.S. and South Vietnamese forces to defensive actions; make a convincing demonstration of its intention to withdraw its forces from Vietnam over a specified period of months; and begin a generous effort to help repair the destruction that has been wreaked upon Vietnam. Nhat Hanh described the plan as "a third way" that did not "pit brother against brother." Among the principle obstacles to peace, Nhat Hanh said, was America's support for "those elements which appear to be most devoted to U.S. wishes for Vietnam's future" rather than the wishes of the Vietnamese people themselves.[3]

Following up on the press conference, the FOR staff arranged a series of meetings for Nhat Hanh with influential figures—key religious leaders, senators and congressmen, editors of the *New York Times* and other major newspapers, and even Secretary of Defense Robert McNamara. A cross-country lecture trip followed. By 1967, Nhat Hanh was becoming widely known as an independent Vietnamese

Press conference in Washington on June 1, 1966

voice representing not only Buddhists but all those who were victims of the war in Southeast Asia.

Wherever he went, Nhat Hanh impressed and disarmed those he met. His gentleness, intelligence, and sanity, plus his fluency in English, made it impossible for most who encountered him to hang on to their stereotypes of what the Vietnamese were like. Not only did his peace proposals make sense, but the vast treasury of Vietnamese culture and Buddhism spilled over through his stories, poetry, and explanations. His interest in Christianity, even his enthusiasm for it, often inspired Christians to shed their condescension toward Nhat Hanh's Buddhist tradition. In the course of his lecture trips, he was able to help thousands of Americans glimpse the war through the eyes of Vietnamese peasants, neither Communist nor anti-Communist, who were laboring in rice paddies and raising their families in villages surrounded by ancient groves of bamboo. After an hour with Nhat Hanh, many who met him were filled with anguish at America's military intervention in the tribulations of the Vietnamese people. No ideology could justify the horror of the skies raked with bombers, houses and humans burned to ash, and children left to face life without the presence and love of their parents and grandparents.

Predictably, Nhat Hanh's peace activities were not appreciated by the U.S.-backed government of South Vietnam. He was denounced as a traitor by several generals, while the Hanoi regime accused him of being pro-American. Warned by friends in Vietnam that he would be in grave danger should be return home, he found himself in exile. What was to have been a three-month absence made him an expatriate for more than forty years.

~

Everything is destroyed

One of the persons Nhat Hanh had long hoped to meet while in the United States was Thomas Merton, the Trappist monk and widely read author who was known for his opposition to war and also for his deep respect for Buddhism. In late May 1966, Merton welcomed Nhat Hanh, plus John Heidbrink of the Fellowship of Reconciliation staff, to the Abbey of Our Lady of Gethsemani in Kentucky for a two-day visit.

The two monks stayed up late into the night in Merton's hermitage, sharing the chant of their respective traditions, discussing methods of prayer and meditation, comparing Christian and Buddhist aspects of monastic formation, and talking about the war.

Merton started their exchange by asking what the war was doing to Vietnam. "Everything is destroyed," Nhat Hanh replied. This was, Merton told the Trappist novices in a lecture a few days later, truly a monk's answer—no long-winded political bla-bla-bla, but the situation encapsulated in just three stark words: "Everything is destroyed. Bang. Period."

They discussed the different religious systems in which they were formed and the importance of building bridges connecting each other's tradition. Monastic formation, Nhat Hanh said, had much to do with discovering the significance of "insignificant" activities: cutting vegetables, gardening, pulling weeds, sweeping floors, washing dishes, waiting in line, walking from here to there, paying attention to day-shaping bells.

Merton was impressed by Nhat Hanh's comment that it doesn't help to rush from a "less sacred to a more sacred" part of the monastery where, once you arrive, you change gears and move more reverently. "Before you can meditate," Nhat Hanh told Merton and Merton told his young novices, "you must learn how to close the door." The novices laughed, aware of how often they ran to the church in order to be on time to chant the monastic offices, leaving behind them a trail of slammed doors.[4]

"Thich Nhat Hanh is a perfectly formed monk," Merton said to his fellow Trappists. He regarded his guest's arrival as an answer to a prayer. "In meeting Thich Nhat Hanh," Merton said, "I felt I had met Vietnam."

before you
can meditate
you must
Learn How
to close
THE DOOR NHAT HANH
AS QUOTED TO
NOVICES BY
THOMAS MERTON

Journal page

"Thich Nhat Hanh is my brother," Merton declared afterward. "He is more my brother than many who are nearer to me in race and nationality, because he and I see things exactly the same way."

A photo I took of Thomas Merton just outside his hermitage

Thomas Merton with Thich Nhat Hanh

~

Martin Luther King Jr.

Another person who immediately bonded with Nhat Hanh was Martin Luther King Jr.

In an encounter arranged by Al Hassler, the two met in Chicago during Nhat Hanh's first U.S. lecture tour.

"Dr. King is not only a brave man but a gifted listener," Nhat Hanh later told the Fellowship of Reconciliation staff. "As with Thomas Merton, you can say just a little

Martin Luther King Jr. and Thich Nhat Hanh

and he understands a great deal. I told Dr. King that many people in Vietnam regard him as a *bodhisattva*. It was a new word for him. I explained that it means someone who is fully awake, like the Buddha."

King nominated Nhat Hanh for the world's most respected honor for opponents of war. "I do not personally know of anyone more worthy of the Nobel Peace Prize than this gentle monk from Vietnam," King said at a press conference with Nhat Hanh. In his letter of nomination he said that the honor would "remind all nations that people of good will stand ready to lead warring elements out of an abyss of hatred and destruction. It would reawaken people to the teaching of beauty and love found in peace."

King added: "Thich Nhat Hanh is a holy man, for he is

humble and devout. He is a scholar of immense intellectual capacity. The author of many published volumes, he is also a poet of superb clarity and human compassion. . . . Thich Nhat Hanh offers a way out of [Vietnam's] nightmare."[5]

∼

Seeking enlightenment and saying no _____

Al Hassler was the staff person who most often accompanied Nhat Hanh wherever he went in America, but occasionally another Fellowship of Reconciliation staff member might have that privilege. One evening I was pressed into the job. Nhat Hanh was waiting for me at an apartment where he was staying near Columbia University.[6] We went by subway to a small gathering at a posh apartment on Park Avenue in midtown Manhattan.

The event we attended turned out to be disappointing. Slipping away at the earliest possible moment, we returned to the street. I suggested perhaps a cup of tea wouldn't be a bad idea. Nhat Hanh agreed. We found a fluorescent-lit Chinese café, and there it was that I decided to ask a question that I thought only a Zen master could answer.

Not many weeks before, while at the University of Oklahoma to give a lecture on Vietnam, I had tried the hallucinogenic drug LSD at the invitation of a member of the chemistry faculty. It was an experiment way off my beaten track, but Aldous Huxley's book *The Doors of Perception* had stirred an interest in consciousness-expanding drugs. At the time LSD was not illegal. It had been described by my chemist friend as triggering "a profound spiritual experience, even a chemical shortcut to enlightenment."

That night-long inner pilgrimage had, in the vocabulary of the sixties, blown my mind. For perhaps ten or twelve hours—in fact I found myself outside of time—I dived into my subconscious brain in which eternity was a reality rather than a concept. I was able to watch a fragment of sound drift slowly into my head and observe how my neurons received that sound and eventually made decisions about it, deciding it was, for example, a syllable of a word or a note of music, a sound to be welcomed or a danger-related noise that required my moving away. Just to hear and decode a simple sentence was a major event experienced in hyper-slow motion. The traffic-directing, sorting-out, editing-room part of the brain was, I found, a bright, colorful, contemplative metropolis methodically making sense of the avalanche of data constantly being provided by my senses, at the same time comparing this with that, taking a fresh look at potentially relevant memories, making wild guesses, considering what response if any might be required to what was going on around me. Slowly emerging from the experience at dawn, I felt I had lived, or was still living, an infinity of lifetimes. It was also an experience of constant awe—of being in the divine presence. Afterward I wondered if indeed this might be enlightenment.

Now I was face to face with one of the few people who would know, but to ask seemed risky. Might a Zen master be scandalized by such a question? How dare I imagine there were chemical shortcuts to enlightenment! What impertinence! But what the hell, I decided—I'll never have another chance to know. And so I asked.

Nhat Hanh's eyes widened in surprise. There was no trace of irritation, only curiosity. Looking back, I think he was astonished that there were people involved in antiwar protest who were interested in enlightenment. "Please tell me what you experienced," he said. I did my best to do so and have rarely been listened to so attentively. When I finished, Nhat Hanh said, "Perhaps it is not enlightenment—no chemicals can do that—but you are on the way." He added that he had once tried marijuana but would never do so again—he had not been able to sleep for days afterward.

There was a deep sense of connection, an almost audible click. Then he asked if in the future I would accompany him on his FOR-arranged travels whenever Al Hassler was unavailable. "If you say yes, you have to be good at saying no," he added. "Every third day for me is a day of mindfulness. On those days under no circumstances will I give any talk or participate in any meeting, no matter how important it may seem. On those days I need someone who can be a stone wall. Can you do that? Others have said they could but in actual practice could not. For them the proposed event was too important. Also I want no more than two events per day on the days between."

"I am good at saying no," I assured him. "I can say no to the president or to the pope. I like the word no."

After that evening we traveled together a great deal, from the East Coast to West and back. I had many opportunities to say no to interview requests, meetings with important people, opportunities that, on any other day, would have been worthwhile. My no was waterproof.

∾

Climbing stairs and mindful breathing _____

It was from Nhat Hanh that I first became aware that walking and attention to breathing both provide opportunities to repair the damaged connection between the physical and spiritual. In conversation Nhat Hanh sometimes had spoken of the importance of what he called "mindful breathing," a phrase that seemed quite odd to me at first. Yet I was aware that his walking was somehow different than mine and could imagine this might have something to do with his way of breathing and also his way of listening. Even if we were late for an appointment, he always walked in an attentive, unhurried way. "Better to be late," Nhat Hanh said, "than breathless. What is most important is to be in the present moment."

It wasn't until we climbed the steps to my sixth-floor apartment in East Harlem that I began to understand. Though quite fit, I was always out of breath by the time I reached my front door. Nhat Hanh, on the other hand, seemed rested. I asked him how he did that. "You have to learn how to breathe while you walk," he replied. "Let's go back to the bottom and walk up again. I will show you how to breathe while climbing stairs."

While I was not thrilled to repeat the climb, on the way back up Nhat Hanh quietly described how he was breathing—a breath in for one step, a breath out for the next, a brief rest on the landings. It wasn't a difficult lesson. Linking slow, attentive breaths with climbing the stairs made an astonishing difference. The climb took a little longer, but when I reached my door I found myself refreshed instead of depleted.

Eyes of compassion _____

I don't recall Nhat Hanh ever giving a talk in which the word "compassion" was not included. "Those who are without compassion," he often said, "cannot see what is seen with the eyes of compassion."

As I gradually came to know him, I began to realize that I and many other peace activists tended to be prisoners on a conveyer belt of activity that often led to burnout, not only due to physical exhaustion but also because of compassion exhaustion. Being attentive to suffering on a daily basis is hard work. Many of us were overwhelmed by a sense of failure and futility. Nor was there much peace in the peace movement. Often we would-be peacemakers were arguing heatedly with one another. Far from loving our opponents and regarding them with eyes of compassion, many of us were glaring at those who supported the war, regarding them as enemies with whom we would never find common ground. It dawned on me that Thich Nhat Hanh could help me, and others like me, acquire a more sustaining form of social activism. So many of us were overlooking something as essential to our lives and work as breath itself.

Breath itself! It was astonishing news that something as simple as attention to breathing could play a significant part in meditation and prayer. It is like a mystery novelist's idea of hiding diamonds in a goldfish bowl put in plain view—a place too obvious, too public, to notice.

I began to be aware that one of the obstacles to entering

a state of mindfulness and meditation is that the opportunities are too close at hand, too ordinary, too prosaic: in the kitchen, on a cutting board, in subways and buses, in supermarket waiting lines, on sidewalks, on staircases, on picket lines . . . literally everywhere. Spending time in places of dedicated silence and stillness, like churches, monasteries, and retreat centers, is helpful but not indispensable. A meditative life doesn't require a hothouse existence, even if it benefits from occasional periods of time when special attention can be given to becoming more mindful.

The way of prayer, meditation, and mindfulness carries to a deeper level the personal disarmament each peacemaker is already attempting while helping ward off inner exhaustion and depression.

"When I was a younger monk, I was sometimes in an unbalanced state myself," Nhat Hanh told me. "There were times I was so focused on stopping the war that I didn't give myself time to notice such simple things as the flowers in front of me. But I learned that if we don't maintain the right balance, we won't be successful and we even increase our own suffering and the sufferings of others."

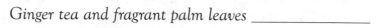

Ginger tea and fragrant palm leaves _____

On the road, Nhat Hanh was always awake before I was. His nights were short. When he decided it was time to wake me, he would sit at the foot of whatever bed or couch I was using and quietly say, "Wake up, Jim! Wake up! Don't you want some ginger tea?" There was a pot of tea in his hand, the perfume smell of fresh-cut ginger in the air, a happy smile on his face and a teasing look in his eyes.

While drinking cups of fresh tea each morning, Nhat Hanh was often reminded of Phuong Boi monastery, a mountain retreat two hundred kilometers from Saigon, which he and several friends had founded in 1957. "*Phuong boi* means fragrant palm leaves," he explained. "We were a small experimental community in the central highlands supporting ourselves by growing tea. We had no rule and there was no dress code—I dressed as I pleased and would go for days without shaving. I was a hobo monk! Each day created its own rule. We tended the tea plants as needed, but for the rest of each day we could study or write or go for a hike or arrange a picnic or rest in a hammock. To be at Phuong Boi was to visit the Pure Land described in Buddhist sutras. We were far from civilization. From footprints they left in the soft earth, we could see that we shared our Pure Land with several tigers, but they must have been Buddhist tigers—we sometimes encountered them but they caused us no harm. There were also tribal people, the Montagnards, living not far away, who sometimes visited us. We drank tea together. But our experiment lasted only three years. Phuong Boi was closed in 1960 when agents of the government arrested one member of the community and forced the rest of us to leave. I returned to Saigon. It was a very sad day but the memories are sweet."[7]

I asked what had led him away from urban life and the many existing monasteries to seek refuge in the mountains. "Each of us had been made to feel unwelcome by the Buddhist hierarchy as it was at that time. The accusation was that I was sowing dissent. I had been editing a magazine, *Voice of the Rising Tide*,[8] that called for the development of a renewed Buddhism more responsive to the needs of the people, but the magazine was closed and our ideas rejected. I realized taking some distance and being quiet would be a wise step."

~

Chopsticks

Almost every evening there was an invitation for us to have a meal with a family that had played a part in arranging whatever Nhat Hanh was doing locally, but with rare exceptions the response I had to make was, "No thank you—Thich Nhat Hanh is too tired." Table conversation, he had explained to me, was too draining. We would be brought to wherever we were staying, say goodnight, and then look for a Chinese restaurant, the simpler and plainer the better.

Our meals were often playful. Nhat Hanh banned the use of knives, forks, and spoons. He wanted me to become at home with chopsticks. Little by little I made headway. He enjoyed making me practice lifting melting ice cubes out of glasses of water. Much laughter.

Thich Nhat Hanh with face drawing on one finger

❀

Greener grass _____

By now Thich Nhat Hanh was becoming "Thay" (pro-
nounced Tie), the Vietnamese word for teacher. He was
certainly a teacher for me, though occasionally the roles
were reversed. Thay had an avid interest in Christianity,
not only as a theory or theology but as a way of life. At
his request, I often told stories about Christian saints
that I held in especially high regard—Francis of Assisi

St Francis of Assisi

and Benedict of Nursia, for example, and the Desert Fathers, who had been the first Christian monks. He was eager to know about Dorothy Day and the Catholic Worker movement, which I became part of after my discharge from the Navy—it had, he said, much in common with the School of Youth for Social Service in Vietnam. We also talked about the Buddha, whose name, Thay explained, came from the Sanskrit verb *budd*—"to be awake." Thay speculated that not only the Buddha but Jesus had become fully awake. "When someone becomes fully awake, the world is changed. The grass is greener, the sky is bluer."

Half smiles

Though his face glowed with a shy, subdued smile most of the time, Thay's face sometimes revealed how difficult was his inner struggle with news of so much suffering touching his daily life. I recall the tears streaming down his face after opening a telegram that bore news of the death in Vietnam of a person especially dear to him. For a long time he stood in silence, gazing out a window into the dark night. Finally he turned to me and said in a whisper, "Nothing is wasted." His usual smile didn't reappear for several days but finally it came back.

"Smiling is not hard work," Thay told me. "It is much easier than frowning. A smile relaxes many muscles and also relaxes your nerves. It makes it easier to breathe and walk mindfully. It makes it easier to be in the present moment." He recommended adopting the half smile as a facial habit. "A half smile is what you see on all statues of the Buddha."

Vietnamese Buddha statue

~

What is Zen?

"Zen" was a much-used word in the sixties, but exactly what it meant was far from clear. Time and time again Thay was asked the question, "What is Zen?"

"Talking about Zen," Thay replied on one occasion, "is like talking about table tennis. You invite me to play but I don't know how. I see paddles are needed and ask how do I handle the paddle? And you tell me how to do it, but your words only confuse me. They are only words. So I just play with the paddle and find out by playing."

Journal drawing. Zen meditation cushion

Yet another answer, this one using the metaphor of music: "Zen is direct contact with the reality of life. Why talk about music when one can listen to it?"

Days later, while he was giving a lecture on Buddhism, the same question was raised. Thay tapped the microphone in front of him. "Zen," he said, "is perhaps this microphone, and if it is not this microphone I do not know what it is. To know what Zen is you must know what Zen is not, and I cannot answer that question. I do not know if it is possible to point out what is religious and what is not. I do not know if the microphone is religious or not religious. A microphone is not a microphone and that is why it is a microphone."

Thay pointed to the table next to him. "Look at this table. The concept of the table in my mind is already very funny, a very dry, distorted image of it. We can say the table is not a table and yet it is a table. We can see an infinite number of non-table elements connect to the table. If I meditate on the table I can see the man who made the table and I can see the maker's father and I can see the bread that the father ate at the table and I see many other things. I can see the whole universe in this table. I draw a line between table and non-table, but the reality is there is no distinction. In using words like table and chair and also Zen, we tend to cut reality into pieces."

Asked what books on Zen he recommended, he replied, "Why read a cookbook when you can eat a meal?"

∽

A clock in place of a crucifix _____

Thay noticed things that I hardly noticed and took absolutely for granted, as happened one day at the University of Michigan. He had been invited to give a lecture on the war in Vietnam, to be followed by a poetry reading. Waiting for the elevator doors to open, I noticed Thay gazing at the clock above the doors. Then he said, "You know, Jim, a few hundred years ago it would not have been a clock, it would have been a crucifix." So simple but so startling a comment. He was right. More than a tool of social coordination, the clock has become a quasi-religious object in our world, a symbol of unity, a collective conveyer belt, a symbol so powerful that it could depose the crucifix.

∽

Are you 21?

One day we were walking in a seedy area of San Francisco, the Tenderloin district, and we passed a sex store with wide windows in which photos were on display of everything a passer-by might have wondered about concerning what human genitals can do. Embarrassed, I pretended I didn't see the store, imagining Thay would do the same. But no. He stopped, calmly gazing at the pornography. Then he pointed to a small sign in the window that read, "You must be 21 years old and able to prove it to enter this store."

"Jim," asked Thay, "are you 21?" I noticed the twinkle in his eyes and realized the question was about the advantages of being a child. "No, I'm not 21." "Good," said Thay. "Neither am I. We don't have to go inside."

Hippie clothing

That afternoon we talked about the hippie subculture in America. In San Francisco, we were surrounded by it much of the time. Thay pointed out that the different clothing worn by hippies was a nonverbal protest, a way of saying "we're getting off the highway—we're on a different path." The hippies were wearing "a manifesto without words." He thought hippie clothing would have even more to say if it included an implicit peace message. "I suggest hippies connect with Vietnam by dressing like Vietnamese peasants. The designs are simple and the fabric inexpensive."

He drew four examples in my journal. "Hippies can make it themselves," he added.

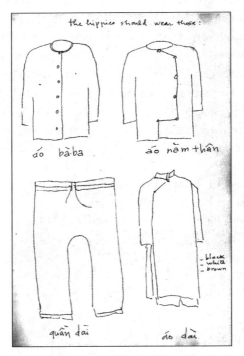

Journal drawing by Thich Nhat Hanh of proposed hippie clothing

～

Meeting a baby bear

One of our trips brought us to Montana, where Thay was a speaker at a university "teach-in" on Vietnam. The event

went well, with about a thousand students and faculty taking part, including a U.S. senator, Walter Mondale, and a
representative from the State Department. But afterward,
because of weather problems, there was a twenty-four-hour
delay of the return flight. Thay welcomed my suggestion
that we use our rented car and the gift of unexpected free
time and visit Yellowstone National Park. Neither of us
had ever been there, and it wasn't far away.

We were lucky to get in—snow plows had just cleared
the main road. Ours was the first car of the day to arrive
at the park's Montana entrance. Once inside, a surprise
awaited us, a sort of welcoming committee: a mother bear
in the deep snow with her two playful cubs. I stopped the
car so we could admire them. Then one of the cubs clam-
bered onto the hood and began licking the window. The
mother bear came closer—she was carefully guarding her
child. Thay began laughing, then kissed the window at the
spot where the cub's pink tongue was engaged.

Bombs away

One evening at a large Protestant church in St. Louis,
where Thay was speaking about what the war was doing to
Vietnamese peasants, a man stood up during the question
period and spoke with searing sarcasm of the "supposed
compassion of this Mister Hanh." He asked, "If you care
so much about your people, Mister Hanh, why are you
here? If you care so much for the people who are wounded,
why don't you spend your time with them?" It was as if

bombs were falling out of his mouth. The stranger's anger became my anger, only directed back at him. When he finished, I looked toward Thay in bewilderment. What could he or anyone say? The spirit of war had suddenly filled the church. It was hard to breathe.

There was a prolonged silence. Then Thay began to speak—quietly, with astonishing calm, even with a sense of personal caring for the man who had just bombarded him. Thay's words seemed like rain falling on fire. "If you want a tree to grow," he said, "it does not help to water the leaves. You have to water the roots. Many of the roots of the war in my country are here, in your country. To help the people who are being bombed, to try to protect them from this suffering, it is necessary to come here."

The atmosphere in the room was transformed. In the man's fury we had experienced our own fury. We had seen the world as through a bomb bay. In Thay's response we had experienced an alternate option: the possibility—brought to Christians by a Buddhist and to Americans by an "enemy"—of overcoming hatred with love, of breaking the seemingly endless counterreactive chain of violence.

But after his response, Thay whispered something to the chairman and walked abruptly from the room. Sensing something was wrong, I left the book table I had been stationed at and followed Thay outside. It was a cool, clear night. Thay stood on the sidewalk at the edge of the church parking lot. He was struggling for air like someone who had been deeply underwater and who had barely managed to swim to the surface before drowning. I had never seen him like this. It was several minutes before I dared ask him how he was or what had happened.

Thay explained that the man's comments had been deeply upsetting. He had been tempted to respond to him with anger. Instead he had made himself breathe deeply and very slowly in order to find a way to respond with calm and understanding. But the breathing had been too slow and too deep.

"But why not be angry with him," I asked. "Even pacifists have a right to be angry."

"If it were just myself, yes," said Thay. "But I am here to represent the Vietnamese peasants. I have to show those who came here tonight what we can be at our best."

~

Dry stone masonry _____

One of our stops was at the Tassajara Zen Mountain Center in a thickly wooded canyon south of San Francisco, a remote place with a stream running through it and a hot spring that Native Americans had used for healing long before Europeans arrived. Here one afternoon Thay and I watched an elderly Japanese monk, a Zen master of the Sōtō school, mindfully gaze at piles of large rocks, no two alike, then carefully feel a few promising stones before at last choosing one and then fitting it, without mortar, into what was becoming the foundation of a new building. It was slow work; but, when a stone was finally chosen and placed, it rested in its new location as if it had forever been intended to be exactly there and nowhere else. Both of us felt blessed to watch. Thay said, "That monk knows what he is doing."

Later in the day I asked Thay if Japanese and Vietnamese Buddhism were similar. "There are differences," Thay replied. "Buddhism in Japan is too nationalistic, too close to the samurai military tradition, with too much sitting on cushions, too much being apart from the world of suffering people. It is not yet engaged Buddhism."

"Buddhism itself," he added, "is like water. It is not Japanese, Chinese, or Vietnamese. As soon as you divide Buddhism into pieces, it is no longer Buddhism."

An altar at the Tassajara Zen Mountain Center

Eating tangerines

One day we sat at a table that had a bowl of tangerines in the middle. I no longer recall what we were talking about, only that I had an idea about something we might do in the future. Perhaps it was a good idea; but, while describing it, I was peeling one tangerine after another and eating the sections as if they were traveling to my mouth on an assembly line. Thay reached out, touched my assembly-line hand and said, "Jim, what are you doing?"

I glanced at the tangerine I was holding. "Eating a tangerine," I replied.

"But have you really noticed it? You ought to eat it section by section, aware of each section. If you pay attention, the tangerine connects with everything, with the sun, with rain and water, with the hands of many people, with the place where its tree was rooted. It has its special taste and color. It helps keep you alive. Pay attention. Wake up. Live in the present moment." Ever since that conversation I think of Thay and what he said whenever I am eating any fruit, but especially tangerines.

Becoming a duck _____

I had a similar experience with rice. We were in a small Chinese restaurant. I had eaten perhaps half the rice in my bowl, pushed it aside and was getting ready to pay the bill and leave for whatever was next on our schedule. Thay pointed to my rice bowl. "Jim," Thay told me, "you will be a duck in your next incarnation." "Why a duck?" I asked. "You have forgotten to finish your rice," Thay responded.

"Every Vietnamese child learns from his mother that no duck ignores even a single grain of rice. If you leave rice uneaten, you will become a duck in your next incarnation and learn to pay attention to each grain of rice."

Killing the Buddha

Thay's responses to questions often surprised me. A student of Buddhism whom we met in Santa Barbara, California, asked what it meant to seek the Buddha and what happens when you find him. Thay answered, "I am a Zen master—and, as you know, Zen masters always reply incomprehensibly. So I will say that you only find the Buddha by killing the Buddha whenever you find him."

Then he laughed and said, "But I am a nice Zen master, so I will tell you that the Buddha is truth and the only thing that keeps you from finding truth is your conviction that you have already found it. So whenever you find truth, you must recognize it is a lie, kill it, and go on in the search for truth. Becoming a bodhisattva—someone fully awake—is not reached via methods or ideologies or study or fasting. Memorizing all the sutras is helpful but will not force open the door. You can sit a thousand hours on a meditation cushion and still be stranded. A diet restricted to green leaves will not assure your entrance into the Pure Land. If you think you have encountered the Buddha, it is more likely that it is only a concept of the Buddha—an idol, an illusion. To encounter the true Buddha, we have to kill that illusion."

(excitement: like hearing many voices coming from downstairs
like the sound of alka-seltzer tablets fizzing
in a glass of water)

EXCITEDLY the SKY GIVES BIRTH TO A
NEW DUSK
the BLUE-eyeD BIRD hops AMONG
CRYSTAL LEAVES,
AWAKENED FROM FORGetFulNESS
MY SOUL GIVES BIRTH TO A DAWN
the LAKE OF MIND SILENTLY ReFLects
A PEACeFUL MOON.

bodhisattva

At every step, A PURE WIND RISES.
EVEN A GOOD thING IISN'T AS GOOD AS NothING.
to GougE out heAlthy FLESh AND MAKE A WOUND.
to COVER ONE'S EARS AND STEAL the BELL.

iN the POT SUN AND MOON ShiNE eteRNALLY.
Once upon a time there was a hermit who always
carried shoes about with him, and a pot that could
hold a peck of rice. At night he spent his sleep within
the pot. Sometimes the pot changed into the universe with
the sun and moon in it. He named the pot "Pot Heaven"
and he himself was known as Mr. Pot.

*Page from my journal. Thay has written the Chinese ideogram for
bodhisattva in the middle section.*

Killing a concept

Wherever we went Thay gave talks—no two identical—and read poems. Whether lecture or poetry or both, the topic of war was always central.

One story that was often included in his talks concerned a brief encounter he had had with an American army officer. Thay had met him on the tarmac of an airfield where he was waiting for a flight that would take him to Da Nang.

"I realized the officer was probably waiting for the same plane. I felt sorry for him—so far from home and his family, so alone, in a country whose language he could not speak, whose customs he did not understand, in the middle of a war in which he might be killed. I said to him, 'You must be very afraid of the Vietcong.' But it was the wrong thing to say. He immediately put his hand on the gun he was wearing. I could see his thought. Perhaps I was a Vietcong! There was panic in his eyes. I realized he had been warned that any Vietnamese person, even a child or a mother, might be Vietcong. 'What are you?' he asked. I had to breathe deeply. 'I am not Vietcong. I am a monk waiting for a plane so I can visit Da Nang. There is a flood there and I have to assess the needs.' I kept my voice very calm. He relaxed and took his hand off his gun. He asked about the flood and what I was doing about it. I was not killed. But what if our meeting had gone differently? What if he had taken his gun and killed me? Would he have killed Thich Nhat Hanh? No. He had never met Thich Nhat Hanh—he had met and killed a Vietcong. He had killed an enemy, a concept, not a person."

the BUDDHA RIDES
ON tHe ISLAND
OF A tURtLe'S BACK
IN tHe WIND
SUCH AS IS NOW POURING
tHROUGH MY LUNGS
AND YOURS

Drawing of the Buddha—a page from my journal

Bomb damage in Vietnam

Tra Loc

More bombs were dropped on Vietnam than were
dropped on all of Europe during the Second World War.
The destruction was unimaginable, the dead uncountable.
In Vietnam, some of the bombs fell on Tra Loc, a village
in which the School of Youth for Social Service was active.
"It was a place of beauty but all the homes were destroyed,"
Thay said. "The young volunteers asked my advice—should
the village be rebuilt? I said yes. It was rebuilt. But then the
village was bombed a second time. Again it was rebuilt.
Three times American bombs destroyed the village, and
three times it was rebuilt. After the third bombing our volunteers and all the surviving villagers were deeply demor-
alized. They thought it was time to give up. But, after
much reflection, I urged that they help rebuild Tra Loc a
fourth time. Otherwise we were surrendering to despair,

our most dangerous enemy. If we give up on Tra Loc village, the war has defeated us. It was a difficult spiritual struggle to rebuild Tra Loc once again, but it was done and so far has been spared."

~

Saying yes

It isn't easy to describe the influence Thay had on me in the course of our travels. Partly it was simply guidance about what I would call being in a state of prayer, and Thay would call it mindfulness or being in the present moment.

In contrast with Dan and Phil Berrigan, good friends with whom I was also working closely, Thay exerted no pressure on me to do more than I was already doing to

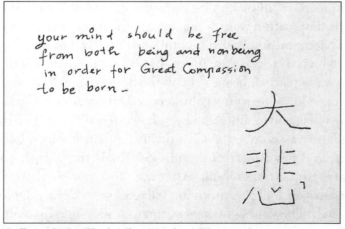

Calligraphy by Thich Nhat Hanh of Chinese ideograms for great compassion

end the war in Vietnam. But because of Thay, Vietnam was no longer a distant country. It was as close as Thay's voice. Its tragedies were mine. I had broken into what Thomas Merton called "the human dimension."

When I was invited to be part of a community that was preparing to impede military conscription by burning draft records, with the probability of a long period in prison as a consequence, part of the reason I said yes was my love of Thich Nhat Hanh and the awareness that Vietnam—though I had never been there except through Thay—was part of my home.

Letter to a prisoner

In September 1968, I was one of a group of fourteen who burned thousands of draft files on a small square in Milwaukee, Wisconsin. During the trial the following spring, we attempted, with some success, to put the war on trial, but in the end we were found guilty, as we expected.[9] While serving a year in prison—1969-70—I received a letter from Thay.

"Do you remember," he asked, "the tangerine we shared when we were together? Your being there is like the tangerine. Eat it and be one with it. Tomorrow it will be no more."

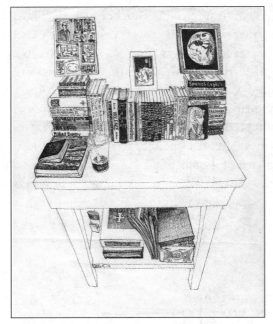

Drawing of the table in my prison cell

A *flight to Paris*

It was July of 1971. No longer in prison, for a year I had been living at Emmaus House, a house of hospitality and community in Manhattan's East Harlem. An invitation came for me, as co-secretary of the Catholic Peace Fellowship, to take part in an antiwar meeting being hosted by the Quaker International Center in Paris. The Emmaus community encouraged me to say yes, and a friend paid for the air ticket.

A major part of my reason for the trip was wanting to see Thay, now based in Paris, where he was head of the Vietnamese Buddhist Peace Delegation, set up by the

Unified Buddhist Church of Vietnam to represent the Buddhists of South Vietnam at the official peace negotiations then underway.

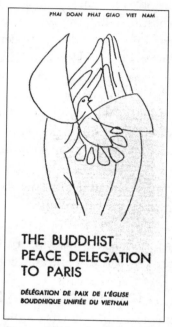

Cover of folder for the Vietnamese
Buddhist Peace Delegation

The Vietnamese Buddhist Peace Delegation: with such an impressive name, I imagined the delegation's offices might be in the diplomatic quarter of Paris. In fact the location proved to be an overcrowded Arab neighborhood not unlike my own district in East Harlem, except here the streets were older, narrower, and twisted. The office, reached by a narrow staircase, was a room with several desks and a view across the rooftops of St. Bernard's Church with its flying buttresses and charcoal black steeple.

Two people were there: Laura Hassler, Al Hassler's daughter, now a volunteer helping with the delegation's work, and Cao Ngoc Phuong,[10] who had been a professor of biology at the Universities of Hue and Saigon and, as a prominent figure in peace actions in Vietnam, was one of Nhat Hanh's principal collaborators. Phuong was wearing a traditional *ao dai*—black silk trousers with a slim brown full-length dress, open along the sides from the waist to the ankles for ease of movement in chairless, couchless houses.

At sunset, Phuong and Laura took me to the community's apartment in Maisons-Alfort near the confluence of the Seine and the Marne in the southeast of Paris. The Parc de Sceaux was in walking distance. In the days that followed I often walked to the park and got to know its imposing population of black swans.

The apartment itself might as well have been in Vietnam—a large room with bamboo mats on the floor, a small corner table covered with books and papers, other books in rows at the floor's edge, an altar, and a neatly blanketed mattress on the floor beneath the windows. No tables or chairs. Off to one side was a compact kitchen. A small room in one corner contained several thin mattresses plus one or two more in the living room. In a closet-sized space there was a toilet, and facing it a bathroom that had been taken over by a mimeograph machine.

Thay was waiting for us. Though it had been several years since we had traveled together in America, our conversations resumed as if we had been apart only a few weeks. I was again struck by his gentle voice and deep calm.

Of my many photos of Thay, this is my favorite. It was taken at the apartment in Maisons-Alfort, Paris.

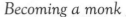

Becoming a monk _____

After supper we had a long conversation about becoming a monk, a vocation he had embraced when he was sixteen. With Thay's permission I recorded it, and other exchanges in the days that followed, using the Sony Walkman cassette recorder I'd brought with me.

"I was initiated into the monastic life by a master," Thay said. "My elder didn't give me things to learn—he just put me into community life. I didn't begin with doctrine. I began by living the monastic life. The very morning I came, they asked me to carry water and work in the gar-

Thich Nhat Hanh as a young monk

den. I was instructed to look carefully at the others, to see the way they do things. By that time I already had received some education of a Western nature, so I thought the kind of education in the monastery was not very advanced, not theory but practice. They gave me simple prayers to memorize. I was annoyed. I felt no one was paying attention to me! But all the time an elder was keeping his eye on me, finding out without words who I was. When he was ready, he began to give me guidance. But first I had to learn patience.

"For instance, he taught me that when you wash your hands, you have to raise in your mind a thought that goes along with washing your hands. You would think to yourself, 'While I wash my hands, I wish that everybody would have clean hands capable of handling the truth.' So whatever you do, you have to become concentrated on it with a thought, and this is how we are trained for meditation. You get stronger concentration of mind. They had me learn things by heart. I thought it wasn't very advanced, but I finally found it very helpful. The most important thing is that they don't want to initiate you with philosophy, theory, doctrine. They want to push you right away into life, into that kind of monastic life. You learn better that way. You learn to be aware of every action, no matter how small."

~

Roots of engaged Buddhism

Another day I asked about the origins of what Thay called "engaged Buddhism."

"In 1964," Thay said, "I returned to Vietnam after a three-year period of study and teaching in the United States. Civil war was raging, and America's role in it was steadily enlarging. Saigon was crowded with refugees. Many monasteries had been damaged or destroyed, including our own retreat in the mountains, Phuong Boi. Where the monasteries had physically survived, the monks had either fled or been forcibly evicted by the Saigon government, which for eight years, until 1963, had been led by an intolerant Catholic, Ngo Dinh Diem. Some monks rebanded into less visible communities while others became active in helping its victims—activities that their critics judged as unmonastic. But in the circumstances of war, helping the suffering was the essential response of any monk, more important than chanting sutras."

"There is really not much division between the two kinds of life, monastic and nonmonastic," Thay explained. "The monastery is like a laboratory. A scientist, if he wants to do his scientific work, has to be in his lab. He has to refrain from such things as smoking, listening to the radio, chewing gum—things like that. It is not because these things are evil. But if you want to work for something, you have to stop doing those things which interrupt your work. So monastic life is a lab in which you work hard to obtain something. It is not an end in itself—it is a means."

Nhat Hanh's words seemed to float on a river of silence.

"Now," he continued, "the essence of Buddhism is compassion and wisdom. But if that compassion and wisdom are not translated into life, it would not be compassion and wisdom! So it is not a problem of speculation. If you have compassion and wisdom and find yourself in a situation of suffering, you will do what your conscience dictates. The only thing we believe is that action should be rooted in a nonaction base, which is the spiritual source of wisdom and compassion. For without wisdom and compassion, action would only further trouble the world. That is why conserving monastic life is so important. But monastic life is also for life. There is really not much separation between monastic and nonmonastic life. The hard thing is trying to find the needed work while preserving your spiritual strength."

Out of his Buddhist "nonaction" base, Thay founded Van Hanh University in Saigon, named for a monk of the eleventh century whose followers initiated a nonviolent movement that resulted in discouraging the Chinese from invading Vietnam. The university, together with La Boi publishing house, also founded by Thay, provided an intellectual and spiritual base for what Thay called "engaged Buddhism."

To supplement the academic format of the university, Thay went on to create the School of Youth for Social Service as a faculty of the university. The school became one of the principal channels for relief and direct action through which increasing numbers of young people found a way to assist refugees, to help in village reconstruction, to set up emergency medical centers, to teach better methods of agriculture and sanitation, and to begin small schools.

"In the late fifties and early sixties, religion was the only institution left that inspired a sense of national unity," Thay explained. "There was the potential for Buddhism to initiate many constructive efforts. But at that time the Buddhist hierarchy had no vision of what to do and turned deaf ears to our proposals. My friends and I had to act on our own—to develop new structures, new projects, new publications. The vision grew out of our period of retreat to the La Boi Hermitage where I did a great deal of writing. Slowly the Buddhist hierarchy began to see our ideas and efforts as helpful. More and more young people volunteered to help us—Phuong was one of them. They were motivated by love and worked without wages. Van Hanh University, next to Phap Hoi Temple, was taking shape in Saigon and became my home. Very quickly the School of Youth for Social Service was born and began working in villages in small teams, launching all sorts of self-help projects—clinics, classes, starting a library, finding clean water. We don't decide what is to be done, but we offer our services. When the villagers ask for help, we try to give it."

Deep sadness

When I had first gotten to know Thay, I had been impressed by his hopefulness. My first impression of him in Paris in 1972 was that much of his hope had wilted. His half smile wasn't always there. I sensed a deep sadness in him, as if he were a rabbi at Auschwitz. There was a clue to this sadness in the room in which we were sitting. Against one wall was a low, black table that served as an altar. On it were a candle, some flowers, the stems of burned sticks of incense, and a photograph of Thich Thanh Van, who, since Thay's departure, had been director of the School of Youth for Social Service. On June 2, shortly before my arrival in Paris, Thanh Van was returning from relief work when his small car was hit by a U.S. army truck. Thanh Van was gravely wounded but was refused admittance to the nearby U.S. Army hospital. Two days later he died. Thousands came to the funeral.

Thich Thanh Van had been Thay's most beloved student and closest friend. Thay was devastated. "He cannot be replaced," he told me later while showing me photos of Thanh Van.

Several Vietnamese friends came to visit the next day. Their conversation explored the question of Thanh Van's next incarnation. It was implicit to all that Thanh Van had reached that rare degree of wholeness in which it would be possible for him to freely choose. All agreed Thanh Van was now a bodhisattva and thus could leave the world of suffering forever and enter the "Pure Land" of complete peace and final liberation. But it was Thay and Phuong's view that Thanh Van would return to the Vietnam of the present and once again share in the nation's agony.

Closed eyes

There was another source of Thay's sadness. Four years before, there had been much interest in the United States in the Buddhists' nonviolent struggle. Many Americans seemed to find a new source of energy for peace work in response to their awareness of what the Buddhists were doing in Vietnam. But now many peace activists seemed indifferent, though the Buddhists' struggle was continuing as intensely as ever. There was criticism of the Buddhists

Thich Nhat Hanh reading a letter

for putting their primary emphasis on obtaining a ceasefire rather than concentrating on the nature and composition of a future government. At least one antiwar periodical had gone so far as to connect the Buddhist movement in South Vietnam to the CIA. Representatives of the Vietnamese Buddhist Peace Delegation had not been invited to several recent international peace gatherings, including the one that had brought me to Paris. Nhat Hanh was, he was told, "politically unacceptable."

So, while many Buddhist monks, nuns, and lay people were in prison cells and "tiger cages" (holes in the ground with bamboo bars over the top) for their campaign to end the war, with thousands refusing to fight, their struggle was yesterday's news in a significant part of the antiwar movement. While a leader of relief and peace work lay dead in Vietnam because there was no room for him in a U.S. military hospital, the peace movement had quietly closed its eyes to the existence of the movement Thich Thanh Van had shared in creating.

Only the rice loves you

Day by day Thay's sorrow began to lift. Not that there hadn't been moments of peace and even happiness, as when I arrived, but a new current gradually returned. I began noticing it during our meals.

Over supper one evening we talked about the broken-grain rice we were routinely eating. It hadn't come from the food market but from a pet store. Broken-grain rice is cheap—it costs less than half the usual price—a big saving in a household that had little money and where nearly everyone had five or six bowls of rice a day. But the man at the pet store was puzzled by these huge purchases. "How do the birds you feed eat so much?" the shop owner asked Phuong. She told us her reply: "Well, they are very big birds." We laughed.

Laura asked Thay to explain a puzzling Vietnamese saying, "Only the rice loves you." At that moment Thay was offering me another bowl of rice. I shook my head—I wasn't hungry. Thay opened his eyes extra wide and said, "Don't you want the rice to love you?" What could I say?

He took my bowl, filled it, and handed it back, saying, "Special delivery!"

We never had an explanation of the proverb, only a question to which I said yes.

~

Salt

A salt shaker on the table led Thay to make a comment about nonviolence: "Nonviolence is like salt. It really is important for cooking, but it doesn't do much good unless it's put into the food."

~

Looking at a dish

After supper the following night, Thay held an empty rice bowl and said, "Jim, think of all the threads that are passing through this bowl. Think of the people who made it. Think of those who taught them their craft. Think of the people who played a part in learning to make a bowl that could last through many meals. Think of the people who dug the clay. Think of the fire that making this dish required. Think of the wood cutters. Think of all the meals that have been served in it. Think of the people who made the meals and of those who taught them their skills. Think of the farmers who grew the food we eat from this bowl. Think of all the light that has brightened this bowl. Think of the water that has washed this bowl, water that has fallen as rain and disappeared into rivers and oceans and risen into the air as clouds and then fallen again as rain. In such thinking you are only beginning to see this bowl. The whole universe is present in this bowl."

On another day Thay laid his finger on the journal page on which I was inscribing a few lines. "If you are a writer, you will see clearly that in every sheet of paper there is a cloud, for without a cloud, there is no rain. Without rain the trees will die—and without trees we have no paper. So we can say that the cloud and the paper exist in a state of interbeing."

∼

Reaching for the moon _____

One night Thay brought a book to me and opened it to a reproduction of an old Zen master's painting: a dead twisted branch coming in from one side, and growing out of it a new and fragile limb, very thin and covered with blossoms. There was no need to know the meaning of the Chinese words, or any words, though Thay did a translation: "The winter plum. / Clearly the morning is coming." In my Christian eyes, it was a way of showing the resurrection: life rising out of death. A simple painting of hope, hope as lived experience, as evident in the gospel of trees as it is in the gospels of words.

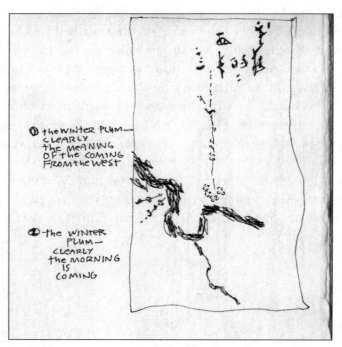

While I was gazing at the Zen painting of the branches, Thay turned the page. No word had been spoken. This time there was a painting of a monkey with large eyes and a face that seemed, in its few brush strokes, full of expectation. There was an oval shape in the water, just beyond the monkey's reach. Thay translated the adjacent Chinese ideograms:

> *The monkey is reaching for the moon in the water.*
> *Until death overtakes him, he'll never give up.*
> *If he'd let go of the branch and disappear in the deep*
>   *pool,*
> *the whole world would shine with dazzling pureness.*

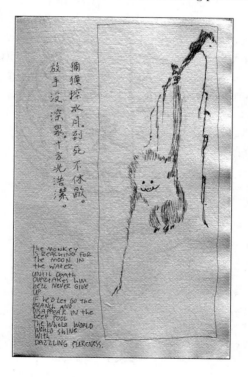

I did a drawing of it, though without the moon reflection. I said to Thay that it seemed to me that I had let go of the branch several times in my life, and several times briefly entered into dazzling pureness. I sensed Thay had let go of the branch once again that day. A new corner in his rebirth process had been turned. The seed had fallen into the ground, died, and now there was a bit of green breaking open the ground's surface. An Easter event.

Hoa Binh

One day Thay cut a potato in two and, using a paring knife, carved two ideographic characters on one half, then used the potato to make a succession of prints. "It is '*hoa binh*,'" Thay explained, "the word for peace written in old Vietnamese before our alphabet was westernized during the French occupation." Read separately, the two ideograms mean "tranquility" and "reconciliation."

The Path of Return _____

Thay showed me the Vietnamese text of a play he had written, *The Path of Return Continues the Journey*. I asked what it was about. "The play is the conversation of the five young people who were active in the School of Youth for Social Service," Thay replied. "All have died. The oldest of them is Nhat Chi Mai, one of my dearest disciples. After graduating from Van Hanh University, she became deeply engaged in School of Youth projects. Then on May 16, 1967, while sitting between statues of the bodhisattva Quan Yin and the Virgin Mary, she burned herself as a peace offering. In letters she left behind she appealed for Catholics and Buddhists to work together to end the war so that people might realize the compassion of the Buddha and the love of Jesus. Nhat Chi Mai was thirty-three years old. The day of her death was Wesak, the celebration of the Buddha's birth."

In the play Nhat Chi Mai comes in a simple boat to receive into the afterlife four fellow School of Youth volunteers who have just been executed, whether by Vietcong or government soldiers is not mentioned—it doesn't matter. As Thay said again and again, "Men are not our enemies— our enemies are the fear and ignorance that make men into enemies. The two opposing armies are two sides of the same coin, the coin of war. If we look at what happened with eyes of compassion, we can see in how many ways the two sides in war resemble each other."

He read aloud the final paragraph from his introduction to his play:

Love enables us to see things which those who are without love cannot see. Who will be gone and who will stay? Where do we come from and where shall we go? Are the other shore and this shore one or two? Is there a river that separates the two sides, a river which no boat can cross? Is such an absurdly complete separation possible? Please come over to my boat. I will show you that there is a river, but there is no separation. Do not hesitate: I will row the boat myself. You can join me in rowing, too, but let us row slowly, and very, very quietly.

While Thay translated into English the entire play, I recorded his words. When I returned to New York, I started a small publishing venture, the Hoa Binh Press. Our second project was the publication of *The Path of Return Continues the Journey*. The translation had been polished by the artist Vo-Dinh who also provided handsome illustrations, including a woodcut portrait of Nhat Chi Mai.[11]

Nhat Chi Mai

Phuong had been one of Nhat Chi Mai's closest friends. They had been together the day before Nhat Chi Mai's self-immolation.

"Did you know that she was planning to burn herself?"

"No. None of us knew. We would have tried to prevent it. But afterward I realized she had been thinking day and night for weeks about what she might do that would open people's eyes."

I asked if her action had made a difference.

"Yes. Many people were deeply shaken. Thousands were there on the day of her cremation—the crowd behind the funeral car stretched five kilometers . . . students, workers, monks and nuns, street vendors. And her sacrifice did open doors between Catholics and Buddhists. We put together a small book containing Mai's letters and poems; and a Catholic priest, Father Nguyen Ngoc Lan, wrote a foreword and then helped circulate the book—a very risky thing to do. Anyone talking about peace was regarded as

Communist by the Saigon authorities. People were being arrested every day. I was arrested one day and only managed to be released by eating the peace petition I had with me before I was searched."

Nhat Chi Mai

A new dawn _____

The next day Thay asked if I would draw a picture in my journal to go with a new poem he had written:

Excitedly the sky gives birth to a new dusk.
The blue-eyed bird hops among crystal leaves.
Awakened from forgetfulness
my soul gives birth to a new dawn.
The lake of mind silently reflects a peaceful moon.

My drawing was of two leaves touching with a large moon rising behind them. Thay was pleased.

"Forgetfulness is a big problem," he commented, "forgetting to be mindful from moment to moment, forgetting to be grateful for each step we take on earth, for each breath of air, forgetting the suffering of starving children, forgetting the devastation of war, forgetting our interconnectedness with all life and thus our collaboration in that suffering." The cure for forgetfulness, he added, is mindfulness. "Mindfulness practice has the immediate result of making us feel happy in the present moment. If we are not happy and serene and peaceful, how can we expect the world to become happy and serene and peaceful?"

∼

The thief-proof moon

One of the writers Thay especially appreciated was Basho, a poet who lived in Japan in the seventeenth century. One of Thay's favorite Basho haikus concerned that which is of utmost value but cannot be taken away:

> *The thief left it behind—*
> *The moon in the window.*

∼

Two trees equal forest

"When I entered the monastery in 1944," Thay recalled, "I was given a small book, *Gathas for Daily Life*, and instructed to memorize it, for it would guide me along the path of Zen Buddhism.[12] For example, while washing your hands you learn to be wholly present as you wash your hands. When I first became a student at the Tu Hieu Monastery, I slowly learned to maintain awareness during all activities—weeding the garden, raking leaves, washing dishes."

The book, Thay added, was written in Chinese. In time he became at home in written Chinese, both classical and modern. In answering my many questions, Thay would sometimes take my journal and draw one or more Chinese ideograms and then explain them.

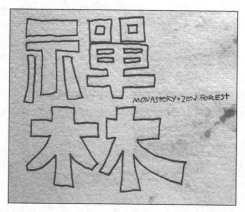

When I asked what the ideogram was for "forest" he made first the ideogram for a tree (a cross with two lines—the roots—descending from the intersection), then made the same sign but joined to the first. "One tree is just a tree—two trees a forest!" Then to the left of "forest" Thay drew the ideogram for "Zen." "Zen plus forest—the combination makes a Zen forest. Together it becomes a monastery. A monastery is a Zen forest. You are already a forest, a *Jim* Forest, but if you achieve zenness, you will become a monastery, a *Zen* Forest."

One day we were talking about trust. Thay drew two ideograms, on the left for "man" and on the right the sign for "word." "Bring these together and you get the sign for 'trust,'" said Thay. "You get a glimpse of the Chinese mentality—the person who keeps his word can be trusted."

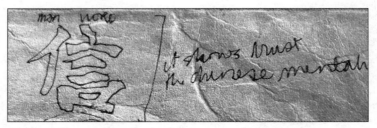

Chinese ideogram for trust

I asked about the ideogram for "mindfulness." "Again it combines two signs," Thay replied, "a mountain shape on the top that means 'now' and beneath it the sign for 'heart.' To have your heart in the present is mindfulness."

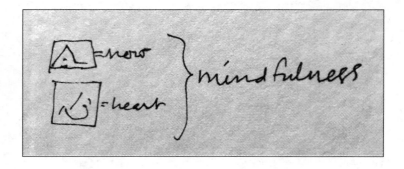

~

Letters from Vietnam _____

However, the new sense of hope, of possibility, didn't dilute the painful words that arrived each day in envelopes from Vietnam. In particular there were detailed reports from a senior nun trying to help refugees coming to Buddhist centers near Hue, fleeing U.S. obliteration bombing in Quang Tri province. B-52 raids were reducing towns and villages to ashes and splinters. Those who were escaping did not dare go to Saigon government refugee camps because these were often the target of attacks from the Vietcong, who didn't want the people to believe Saigon could offer them security, even as refugees. But the Buddhist centers—schools, pagodas and monasteries—while being relatively safe from bomb and mortar attacks, had nothing to offer materially other than what could be begged door to door in the city.

One Sunday morning, another letter from the nun arrived. There were now 15,000 people, she said, 3,000 more than reported in the previous week's letter. Still there was no rice or tins of condensed milk for the infants.

B-52 unloading bombs over Vietnam

In the same mail came another letter. It bore the return address of a large religious relief organization. The letter's author, though expressing regret for the refugees' difficulties, suggested that the problem be referred to another staff member. "Could you write so-and-so?" he suggested. In fact, Phuong had written so-and-so weeks earlier. It had been his suggestion to address the present correspondent.

Vietnamese mother and children escaping attack

"I am really angry," Thay said. His voice was quiet, but the words shook. He held the agency's letter in his hand. Scattered on the floor were photos that had come with the nun's letter. There was a picture of the tents in which the refugees were staying; others were of a mass funeral. One photo that I cannot forget was of an old woman wandering aimlessly, one trouser leg rolled up. Though the woman had lived her many decades in a very modest culture, she had forgotten or lost her shirt. Much of her hair was gone. Before losing her sanity, she had stood for days in an underground shelter up to her chest in water as the earth shook continuously with the explosion of bombs. All the old woman's relatives had been killed, the nun had noted on the back of the photo. Now, though being cared for in a refugee center, she was wandering with vacant eyes calling the names of her dead children.

"Vietnamization"

Soon afterward news of another harsh blow was received: the Saigon regime had ordered that Buddhist monks between the ages of eighteen and forty-three be drafted into the army. They had become monks, it was charged, purely to avoid conscription. In several areas pagodas and

other Buddhist centers had been surrounded by police, and monks were being taken away at gunpoint. It was a new step in the "Vietnamization" of the war, a favorite term of U.S. presidents and generals in the war's last few years.

Meanwhile, bombs continued their work of destruction. I made a drawing in my journal of a photo published in a French magazine that showed the pulverized ruins of a village or town in which by chance a fragment of a Buddhist temple had survived—the altar and the statue of the Buddha sitting in the lotus posture beneath a splintered roof. I was reminded of Basho's poem: "The thief left it behind—the moon in the window." How about: The war left it behind—the Buddha on the altar.

~

Two shores or one shore

Thay often spoke of the problem of dualism—seeing in a way that divides rather than unites. Sometimes he used the image of one river/two shores as a way of attacking dualistic perception. I made what he said into a poem:

> *Standing on a river bank,*
> *I see two shores,*
> *the shore I am standing on*
> *and, on the other side of the river,*
> *the shore facing me.*
> *Two shores.*
> *I see them with my own eyes.*
> *Two!*
> *But in reality there is only one shore.*

If I walk from where I stand to the source of the river
and continue round that point,
the other side becomes this side.
The two-ness is created only by bending the one-ness.
Walk the edge of the stream to its source and keep going
and before long I am on the opposite embankment
facing the spot where I once stood
but I will never have crossed the stream to get there
I will never have changed shores.

I remembered Thay's words in his preface to *The Path of Return Continues the Journey*:

"Is there a river that separates the two sides, a river which no boat can cross? Is such an absurdly complete separation possible? Please come over to my boat. I will show you that there is a river but there is no separation. Do not hesitate. I will row the boat myself. You can join me in rowing too. But let us row slowly and very, very quietly."

Thich Nhat Hanh with co-workers, Paris 1974

Tear-stained letters

So it went. The conference that had been my reason for coming to Paris was long over and, in any event, had been peripheral. For me each day was shaped by Thay and Phuong reading aloud the post from Vietnam. Events half a world away were no longer simply black type on newsprint or gray images on a television screen. The news came to us in handwritten letters that often were stained with tears.

Even though the grief of the first week or two had lifted and we were able to laugh with each other over meals and eat more bowls of "special delivery" rice, there were still nights when I watched tears slipping down the side of Phuong's face as she lay under the window on the blankets, staring at the ceiling.

Phuong

Buddha's robe

After supper one evening, Phuong sang several Vietnamese songs. She has a nightingale voice. I told her she was the Joan Baez of Vietnam. She blushed, then asked if she might tell a traditional Vietnamese story. I eagerly agreed.

"At one time Vietnam was greatly troubled by the evil doings of Mara, the tempter. There was much struggle and discord. It seemed nothing could stop the endless conflicts. Then one day the suffering of the people became known to the Buddha. He decided to negotiate with Mara. 'You can have our land to torment as you please,' said the

Buddha. 'Only would you agree to leave one small spot where we can live in peace?' Mara was suspicious. 'How much land do you want?' Mara asked. 'Just a piece no bigger than my yellow robe,' said the Buddha. Mara readily agreed—he had expected a demand for much more—and promised not to touch the area covered by the Buddha's robe. But when the Buddha took off his robe and unfurled it, it stretched to the north and south, to the east and west, covering all the land that was habitable and arable. All of Vietnam came under the protection of the Buddha's yellow robe. Mara fled into the forests. The Buddha made only one request of the people he had rescued from Mara. He asked them to plant a bamboo in front of each house, and at the lunar new year, Tet, to hang a yellow banner by their door as a reminder to Mara that this is Buddha's land and Mara is not welcome."

Altar drawing

"What a wonderful story," I said, "but then how do we explain the current war?"

"One year a single family, ignoring Tet, forgot to put a yellow banner by their door, and Mara returned to Vietnam."

$\sim$

Jim will answer

One evening Daniel Ellsberg, his wife, Patricia, and son Robert came to visit. Thay asked Dan questions about the release of the Pentagon Papers and what had given him the courage to risk spending many years in prison. Dan said that there had been many factors, but one of the most important had been hearing a young man explain to a university audience why he was awaiting arrest for refusal of military service and was anticipating a five-year sentence. "Courage is contagious," Phuong commented.

Then Dan had a question of his own to ask Thay: "Can you explain Zen Buddhism to me?" Thay smiled, turned toward me with a glance of mischief, and said, "Jim will answer that question." My eyes must have widened in astonishment and my face turned red. I knew practically nothing! Anything I said would have been ridiculous. Thay laughed and said, "Jim's silence is the best answer." As for Thay, he gave no explanation, but he did remark, "It is better to look into the eyes of a Zen master than to read all the books."

$\sim$

Children first

"Please stay longer," Thay said to me each time I spoke of returning to America. "There are many ways you can help." In the end I stayed for a month, but it was finally Thay who convinced me to leave—not because of anything he said but by his example of putting children first. Vietnamese refugee families living in or near Paris often came to visit. What impressed me most during these encounters was how quickly and with what enthusiasm Thay bonded with the children. No adult guest was more important. Watching him connect so unreservedly to our youngest visitors, it dawned on me that my eight-year-old son Ben, living with my mother in New Jersey, needed me and I needed Ben and that I was on the wrong side of the ocean. It was a painful realization—I felt so happy to share in the life of this small Vietnamese island in Paris. The last thing I wanted was to leave. But first things first. I flew back to America.

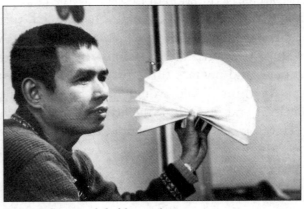

Thich Nhat Hanh holding a fan

~

Quan Yin

On the day of departure the community had a parting gift for me, a small wooden statue of a figure wrapped in a long, flowing robe that seemed shaped by the wind. "She is Quan Yin—*Avalokiteshvara* is her Sanskrit name," Thay explained. "She is the bodhisattva of compassion. Compassion flows from deep attentiveness, deep listening. There are countless bodhisattvas—all are revered—but there is especially intense devotion to Quan Yin. Her name is short for *Guanshiyin*—Quan Yin—which means 'The One Who Perceives the Sounds of the World.' Many people think of her as a god but she is fully human. Like the Buddha, she lived and died. She achieved enlightenment while listening to the sound of a bell and so she is often shown holding a small bell in her hand, but in some images she has many arms, each hand holding some special object. This is to show that the response the com-

Quan Yin statue

passionate person makes in a given situation is unique to that moment and to that particular need. She always finds a way to be with those who are suffering, but there is no standard response. Wherever a compassionate response to suffering is occurring, we can say Quan Yin is present."

I could see in Quan Yin an Asian sister to the Virgin Mary.

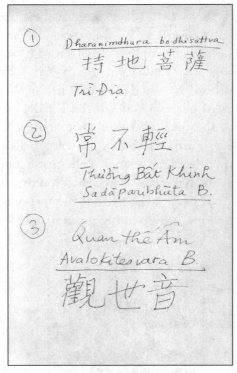

The names of three bodhisattvas as written by Thay

Sweet Potatoes

In 1975, the year the war ended, the community's main base shifted from Paris to a farmhouse near Fontvannes, a village west of the city of Troyes. The community's new encampment was given the cheerful name *les Patates Douces*—the Sweet Potatoes.

"The shift to Fontvannes was a result of being cut off from virtually all communication with our friends in postwar Vietnam," recalls Mobi Warren, a long-time volunteer and translator of some of Thay's books. "Sometimes a telegram would be received from Vietnam that relayed information in code, such as remarking that Uncle So-and-So was doing well, when in fact Uncle So-and-So had been dead for years—a code message that the situation in Vietnam was dire. Another time I remember someone who had been able to flee Vietnam delivered a hand-sewn quilt in which information had been concealed by being sewn between the quilt's layers. By taking the quilt apart, Phuong was able to read the messages. Fontvannes became a place of healing, gardening, and living mindfully while seeking new ways to assist friends in Vietnam."

When I visited Fontvannes in June 1976, Mobi had returned to America several months before. The principal residents at the time were Thay, Phuong, and Sudarat, the last a young woman preparing for work in Thailand modeled on what the School of Youth for Social Service had been doing in Vietnam.

The community life had a monastery-like quality. I was reminded of the Benedictine motto: *Ora et Labora*—Prayer and Labor.

The labor they were doing was of several kinds.

There was a half-acre garden, the community's primary source of food, which included carrots, onions, cabbage, various herbs, spinach, and tomatoes. A head of freshly picked lettuce was on the table at both the afternoon and evening meals. And such lettuce!

It was impressive to watch Thay tend the garden. Under the hot sun he wore a broad Mexican sombrero rather than the conical hat that Asian farmworkers rely on. That summer, work in the garden was more demanding than usual as Europe was suffering the worst drought in more than a hundred years. One night I found Thay watering plants under the moonlight—the water pressure, he explained, was stronger in the middle of the night than during the day.

There was also the ongoing labor of rebuilding what had been a barely habitable ruin when they had first found it. In such decrepit condition, it had been extremely cheap. Little by little the community had done remarkable things in rehabilitating the house. The floors were no longer earthen but cement and, over that, a layer of linoleum. In Vietnamese fashion, there were also several raised platforms covered with bamboo mats or rugs. The plumbing was new. Though it wasn't needed during those hot days, the fireplace was repaired and ready for winter. There was also a meditation room with a small altar over which hung an image of Quan Yin. At the other end of the house a kitchen and bathroom had been added two years earlier. These adjacent rooms had a flat roof, unlike the steep tiled roof over the rest of the house. The attic had been divided into two sleeping rooms.

My son Daniel walking up a path next to the Sweet Potatoes farmhouse

~

La Boi Press

The community's main project at the time was the La Boi Press, named after the type of leaf on which the teachings of the Buddha were first written down. The La Boi Press had actually been founded twice. Until its suppression by the Saigon government, it had been one of the principal elements of the movement for engaged Buddhism that Thay had initiated. All of Thay's books of prose and poetry had been published by La Boi, though several under pseudonyms after the banning of his writings. (One of the ironies of the war was that La Boi publications were also prohibited by the Hanoi-backed National Liberation Front.)

La Boi Press was housed in a former stable that, following renovation, served both as a printing shop and, at night, as Thay's sleeping room. His narrow bed was a thin foam mattress adjacent to a few bookshelves. A printing press stood next to the main door. Here and there were boxes of virgin paper. Nearby was a large cast-iron paper trimmer that looked like an old Franklin press. Other equipment included an old typesetting machine, a device for making lithographic plates for the press, and, in any available ribbons of space, stacks of printed pages waiting to be collated and books stacked under weights while the glue dried. Old yogurt jars served as glue pots, with battered toothbrushes sticking out of them that were used for applying glue.

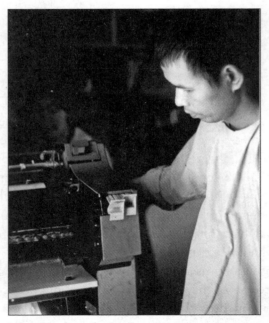

Nhat Hanh at the La Boi printing press

In contrast with La Boi's primitive technology, commercial editions of books are normally printed on large sheets, thirty-two pages to a side, then machine folded and trimmed into sixty-four-page "signatures." The signatures are then machine collated and bound in a very rapid process. The equipment is costly but the cost per copy low and production fast.

Among the books published at Fontvannes was Thay's groundbreaking introduction to mindfulness, originally titled *The Miracle of Being Awake*. Mobi Warren had done the English translation, the first edition of which was initially issued in an edition of sixty copies, which were mailed to friends. (After returning to Nyack from France, I submitted the text to Beacon Press in Boston. It was accepted, renamed *The Miracle of Mindfulness*, and has been a bestselling book ever since, never falling out of print. A few years ago Beacon issued a handsome gift edition.)

Cover of the original edition of Miracle

Current cover of the Beacon Press edition

For each book, Phuong set the type and made the plates for the press. The printing was done by Thay on letter-size A4 stationary—two A5 pages to a side. With its 120 pages, *Miracle* required sixty plates. To do a printing of 350 copies, Thay stood at the press for at least two days. Printing was really the easiest part of the process. Collating the sheets by hand came next—sixty piles of sheets spread out on the floor, then gathered in batches of five or six copies at a time. The backs of the books were scored with a hack saw, demanding but necessary physical labor as the grooves improved the holding strength of the glue. Then came the actual gluing of the pages, the addition of the cover for each book, and finally the trimming. The finished product was attractive and the out-of-pocket expense minimal. Despite their extremely limited financial means and small print runs, the community had built up a catalogue of fifteen titles, an extraordinary accomplishment for a few unhurried people with many other tasks.

When I gave Thay the first copy of the Beacon Press edition of *The Miracle of Mindfulness*, he reminded me that there was still one other title he had almost assigned to the book: *The Miracle Is to Walk on Earth*. "Christians remember that Jesus walked on water, which certainly was a miracle," Thay explained, "but it is also a miracle to walk on earth, to make peace with the earth with each mindful footstep."

Thay's hope was that, over time, La Boi's publishing work would not only be useful and encouraging to Vietnamese exiles but that respect for their work might emerge from the Vietnamese government as it realized, at last, the constructive and reconciling purpose of socially engaged Buddhism. I was impressed by Thay and Phuong's almost miraculous ability to remain hopeful even in the face of what many would judge a hopeless situation.

In fact, shortly after my first visit to the Sweet Potatoes community, Phuong went to Paris in response to an invitation to discuss "national affairs" with the Vietnamese ambassador. She had no idea what had prompted the invitation but went in the hope that, at last, there would be news that the Buddhists could renew their work with Vietnamese orphans and others in desperate need. Phuong harbored the hope that eventually she and Thay would be allowed to return home. She brought the ambassador a newly printed copy of *Phep La Cua Su Tinh Thuc* (*The Miracle of Being Awake*) as well as herbs grown in the Sweet Potatoes garden from seeds sent by monks in Vietnam. While none of Phuong's hopes for the encounter were realized at the time, at least the meeting indicated that Nhat Hanh's community remained on Hanoi's radar screen.

Orders for La Boi books were received daily from Vietnamese refugees in France. The bigger challenge for Thay and Phuong was finding channels to get La Boi books into Vietnam, as the censorship of mail was rigorous. In postwar Vietnam, anything religious was a target. As the state's official cultural publication, *Van Boa Nghe Thuat*, reported in its first issue of 1976, the "new colonialists"—the Americans—used religion as a weapon, spreading "pessimistic thought." "The reactionary anti-Communist band, disguised as religious people, have worked actively in the cultural field, using such slogans as 'actualized religion,' 'bringing religion to life,' 'the religion of the poor' . . . adapting religion to the American puppet policy."

The place of religion in postwar Vietnam was strictly limited to "cultic activities"—rituals inside designated religious buildings. No books about "engaged Buddhism" were permitted, and nothing that implied criticism of the postreligious society.

~

Candy factory

Adjacent to the farmhouse another building was under construction, a rectangular enclosure connected to the kitchen. Two local villagers were helping with this, along with Thay and Sudarat. Sudarat was particularly excited about the project because she wanted to be able to build houses in Thailand. She had quickly become skilled in basic masonry. The new structure would hold tools and equipment, provide storage space for paper and La Boi books, plus space for another cottage industry, making *keo me xung*, a candy traditionally made in Hue and beloved by Vietnamese. Already the community was producing batches of the candy once or twice a month. In each small box they inserted an explanation about *keo me xung*, telling how they sing while making the candy and why the "company name" they had chosen for *keo me xung* was *La Maison de la Demi-Sourire*, the House of the Half Smile, the half smile being an element of the community's meditative practice. The insert encouraged the *keo me xung* eater to read Nhat Hanh's manual on mindfulness, *The Miracle of Being Awake*. Thus even these small projects of self-support became vehicles of teaching. In a more subtle way, there was Buddhist teaching on the box itself: a color woodcut of a leaping fish gazing at the reflection of the moon in the water.

~

Repression in postwar Vietnam

Thay and Phuong shared reports with me of systematic repression in postwar Vietnam—letters smuggled out by friends and also a sober *Le Monde* overview written by an unlikely source, Jean Lacouture, who had been one of the most Hanoi-sympathetic journalists reporting on the war. But in his postwar accounts from Vietnam, Lacouture wrote "one cannot speak so well of the victors," for while the Hanoi authorities had never ceased to reaffirm their commitment to reconciliation and national accord while the war was being fought, in postwar Vietnam no one was

allowed a public voice or a public role or access to a printing press who hadn't proven to be completely loyal to the
government and its ideology. Lacouture estimated that
300,000 people had been placed in "re-education camps."

"The number seems very strong," Lacouture wrote, "and
is difficult to explain. The army of one million soldiers
included only 35,000 officers. Of these . . . most escaped by
sea or land in April 1975, along with 2,000 or 3,000 cadres
of the 'special forces' who were responsible for the bloody
'Operation Phoenix,' all carefully brought out by the Americans. More than a thousand persons with international
relations were also able to escape to other countries. That
leaves only 25,000 former officers to be 're-educated.' So
we can suppose that civil servants can also be arrested—
middle or high-ranking functionaries, politicians, profes-
sors, liberal intellectuals—a very large number, yet even so
it is not easy to achieve the 300,000 figure. . . . But the
silence of the leaders [in Hanoi] when questioned ('It is a
military secret') invites us to keep the [300,000] estimate.
In any event, we can see for ourselves the long line of families of detainees who wait in Saigon—wives and daughters
of the 're-educated' who begin crowding together at dawn
in front of the Central Post Office to send a monthly pack-
age to those who are in 'well-behaved camps' or are 'good
students'. . . . The revolutionary leaders speak much of for-
giveness. It's true that they may be the first victors of civil
war (infected by foreign intervention) who have responded
to their former opponents without massive reprisals . . . but
never have we had such proof of so many detainees."

While some of the camps' inmates might have counted
themselves fortunate not to have been executed as war
criminals in the bloodbath America had predicted in the

event of Communist victory, the shocking fact was that many peace activists who had been imprisoned by the Saigon regime, including Buddhist monks, now suffered a similar fate under Hanoi's administration.

The most distressing document Thay and Phuong turned over to me was a report of the self-immolation of twelve monks and nuns before their monastery altar in Can Tho province. The twelve hoped their sacrifice would inspire the government "to respect all religions." Their action, the abbot explained, expressed "the hope that the blind will see, the deaf will hear, and all living beings benefit." Photos of the twelve came with their letter. I was particularly touched by the photo of the oldest nun, Thich Nu Dieu Phuoc, her face heavy with grief.

Thay and Phuong proposed that I enlist prominent American antiwar activists in making an appeal to Hanoi

Thich Nu Dieu Phuoc

to open the camps to the Red Cross and Amnesty International. "These are people the Hanoi leaders know and whose voices they respect," said Thay.

The appeal I drafted after my return to the United States included these key paragraphs:

> Beginning soon after the victory of North Vietnam and the Provisional Revolutionary Government in the Spring of 1975, and sharply increasing in recent months, reports have reached us indicating grievous and systematic violations of human rights by your government. The evidence is too specific and persuasive for us to ignore. Especially with regard to those imprisoned or otherwise detained, in May a Vietnamese official stated that 200,000 were being held in re-education camps while some respected foreign journalists in Vietnam have estimated 300,000 detainees. The actions of your government constitute a great disappointment to all those who expected . . . an example of reconciliation built on tolerance. We realize that those held include individuals responsible for aspects of the war and the repressive mechanisms of the former Saigon government. But, having believed your fervent past expressions of commitment to human rights, we are deeply saddened to hear of the arrest and detention of a wide range of persons, including religious, cultural and political figures who opposed the Saigon government despite considerable personal risks . . . [various names were cited].
>
> We therefore call upon you to honor the concern for human rights which you have expressed

both in formal agreements and in countless conversations with peace activists. We call for a complete public accounting of those detained or imprisoned indicating, as well, the charges for which they are held. We call on the government of Vietnam to facilitate on-the-spot inspection by the United Nations, Amnesty International, the International Red Cross or other independent international agencies in order to assure that those in the government's charge are treated in accord with international covenants regarding human rights. We call on you to release any individuals who are held purely because of their religious or political convictions. We call for government recognition of the right to open and free communication.

The appeal was co-signed by ninety prominent war resisters but, to Thay's disappointment, many others refused to join the appeal. As a messenger of unwelcome news, I was the target of intense criticism, even accused of being a CIA agent. During the acrimonious months in which debate raged, it became increasingly clear how divisive the issue of human rights can be. People who had marched hand in hand in antiwar demonstrations, and even shared the same cell for acts of resistance, found themselves furiously at odds when confronted with reports of systematic human rights violations in postwar Vietnam. To see, or not to see. . . .[13]

Hanoi never opened its detention centers to any international agencies.

∿

Buddhist mouse traps

The house in Fontvannes was home not only to the Sweet
Potatoes community but to quite a few resourceful mice
who were adept at finding ways to help themselves to rice
and other food supplies. The mice were expensive guests.
A long-running effort to reduce their numbers led to the
deployment of several "Buddhist mouse traps." This non-
injurious device could hardly have been simpler: an upside-
down bowl sheltering a little mouse-appealing food, and a
small stick to hold up the bowl's lip high enough for a hungry mouse to slip inside. The smallest jiggle was enough
to close the opening so there would be no escape. Many a
startled mouse was transported to a nearby forest to be set
free, but Thay and Phuong often wondered if, after depor-
tation, some of the mice hadn't made the journey back to
Sweet Potato heaven. They seemed so entirely at home.

~

A place to sit, a path to walk

In the Sweet Potatoes community, mindfulness exercises
were a basic element of daily life. These weren't something
to be done only when there was some spare time.

The community had tea together each night at about
10:30 and half an hour later began meditative sitting in
a room lit by a single candle. Such sitting ought to leave
the individual feeling deeply refreshed, Thay explained, if
one sits comfortably and quietly while following the body's

breathing and not being attached to passing thoughts or moods. The sitting lasted about forty minutes, with Thay's quiet chanting alternating with the ringing of a sonorous bell and ending with a silent walk inside the house when it was too dark or cold, but outside when the moon was bright and the air comfortable. There were occasional daytime walks as well when we wandered into nearby fields of corn and sunflowers. On one sunny day we cut the stalks of several sunflowers and carried them in a playful procession.

Thay holding a sunflower at Sweet Potatoes

Getting into the Stream _____

After supper one evening Thay helped me better understand the last part of a poem, "Getting into the Stream," that he had written in Paris in 1972 and which I had at the time helped him translate into English:

Each monk has a corner of the mat,
a place to sit
for meditation.
There, monk, sit still on it.
The spinning earth carries us all along.
The place you sit is like a seat on a second-class train.
A monk will eventually get off at his station
and his place will be dusted for another.
How long is the monk to sit in the lotus position
at his corner of the mat?
Sit still on it anyway.
Sit as if you were never going to give it up,
as if there were no station to arrive at.
The engine with its flames will carry you along.
Each monk will sit in the lotus position
at his corner of the mat.
The monk will sit like an ancient enormous mountain.
The mountain is still there,
but like the monk is on the turning earth.
This train of ours,
this fire-filled engine,
is hurrying ahead.
This morning
the monk sits as usual
on his corner of the mat,

but he grins.
"I shall not sit here forever,"
he tells himself.
"When the train arrives at the station
I will be elsewhere —
a corner of the mat
or an armful of grass.
I am sitting down
just one more time."

"Enlightenment is irrevocably initiated when you get into the stream," Thay explained. "For the Buddha, the endpoint of being carried along in the stream, to the point of being beyond birth and death, came when he decided to sit one more time and, even if he should die and rot on the spot, not get up again until he got it. A buffalo boy saw him getting ready to sit and was filled with awe at the Buddha's beauty. He gave the Buddha a gift—a handful of grass. The Buddha sat through the

night on that grass. On seeing the morning star before dawn the next day, his illumination occurred. The point of no return was reached."

One evening, despite a throbbing headache, exhaustion, and the temptation to find a dark corner and lie down, I sat with the community and got up an hour later feeling as if I had been drinking fresh water from a mountain stream. Random thoughts had come and gone during the time. I had frequently strayed into mental noise and the mind's calendars and bulletin boards, yet I found myself letting go of distractions. I noticed them, sometimes glanced at them as if at postcards. Some were interesting but I let all of them go. When the meditation bell rang to mark completion, it seemed much too soon. I wanted to keep sitting. But we walked out into the garden, each following a different path, feeling the bricks of the pathway, enjoying the grass pushing up through the crevices, seeing the moonlight on the lettuce. I found myself silently singing a Gregorian alleluia.

~

Interbeing

In 1966, shortly before his exile from Vietnam, Thay had formed the Tiep Hien Order—the Order of Interbeing. Its initial six members, all board members of the School of Youth for Social Service, were the forerunners of what Thay called "engaged Buddhism."

While staying in Fontvannes, Thay asked me to help him make a translation of the Order's rule. With the Vietnamese text in hand, he read it to me in his own English. I wrote down what he said, then polished it lightly while trying to preserve Thay's voice. Thay then produced a corrected version. The method wasn't ideal, but Thay was pleased.[14]

One of the Order's fourteen rules disarmed all who took the vows: "Do not kill. Do not let others kill. Find whatever means possible to protect life and prevent war." Another required day-to-day mindfulness of the suffering of others: "Do not avoid contact with suffering or close your eyes before suffering. Do not lose awareness of the existence of suffering in the life of the world. Find ways to be with those who are suffering, including personal contact, visits, images, and sounds. By such means, awaken yourself and others to the reality of suffering in the world."

I asked about the term "interbeing."

"It means," said Thay, "that each is in the other. Between us there is no border. In Buddhism we have a term that means interpenetration, but I prefer interbeing. Interpenetration presupposes that there is a border between us but that we can create a door. Interbeing means the door is already there and was always there. We inter-*are*!"

I was reminded of a similar affirmation in the writings of Thomas Merton. In a letter to Amiya Chakravarty, an Indian philosopher, poet, and scholar, Merton wrote, "We all stand on the hidden ground of love."[15] And while speaking at an interreligious congress in India shortly before his death in 1968, Merton said, "The deepest level of communication is communion. It is wordless. It is beyond words, and it is beyond speech, and it is beyond concept. Not that we discover a new unity. We discover an older unity. My dear brothers [and sisters], we are already one. But we imagine that we are not. What we have to recover is our original unity. What we have to be is what we are."[16]

Child visitor with Thay and myself at Sweet Potatoes

∽

Cooking with Nhat Hanh

In the early 1980s Thay came to Holland several times to lead retreats, including a very small one at our house in Alkmaar for the staff of the International Fellowship of Reconciliation. It was the occasion of my wife Nancy's first meeting with Thay. Here is her account:

I came to the Netherlands in April 1982 with my daughter Caitlan, then five years old. Jim and I were married shortly after that. We had been friends for many years in the U.S. Jim was

Cait's godfather. Both of us had worked together at the headquarters of the Fellowship of Reconciliation in Nyack, New York. In 1977 Jim had moved to Holland to serve as general secretary of the International Fellowship of Reconciliation. We had kept in touch during those five years.

Soon after my arrival Jim told me Thich Nhat Hanh would be coming to Alkmaar to visit and also to lead a retreat with the IFOR staff. I had never met Nhat Hanh, but of course I had heard a great deal about him and I knew how close Jim and Nhat Hanh had been over the years.

It was a beautiful day in May. First the staff arrived and seated themselves on our living room floor. Soon afterward Nhat Hanh arrived, dressed in his brown robe. A hush fell over the staff members. Everyone was obviously in awe of this man. I felt nervous that he was coming to our house, nervous about hosting this event.

After he sat down, the room fell silent. A sort of "Zen silence" filled the room. It was hard for me to tell what to make of the atmosphere in the living room that day. I felt uncomfortable. I had never seen the IFOR staff so sedated! Who had these gregarious people become?

In the meantime, Cait, who had just been given her first bicycle, was practicing riding it in the parking lot behind our house. She kept running in to tell me how she was advancing. My attention was divided—on the one hand Thay teaching a roomful of awestruck adults and, on the other, Cait running in, breathless with excitement, announcing her progress in biking. I was torn. The retreat seemed unreal. The IFOR staff seemed to have become instant monks.

Hours later, with the retreat drawing to a close. Jim whispered to me that Thay had agreed to stay for dinner. This was a little more than I could handle—the retreat, Cait and her bike, and

*Thay leading a retreat for IFOR staff at
our home*

now a meal to prepare for a distinguished guest! Leaving the
retreat, I went into the kitchen, closed the door, and started chop-
ping vegetables.

Shortly afterward, Nhat Hanh came into the kitchen and
immediately started helping me with the vegetables and talking
to me in the most ordinary way. He ended up teaching me how to
make Vietnamese rice balls—how to grind the sesame seeds in a
coffee grinder, to make the balls with sticky rice and to roll them
in the ground sesame seeds. It was lots of fun. We laughed a lot!
The artificial Zen atmosphere in the living room—or so it had
seemed to me—was gone. Cait kept coming in and Nhat Hanh
was delighted with her and went out to admire her biking.

This was my first Zen lesson.

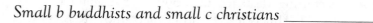

Small b buddhists and small c christians

"Small *b* buddhists can talk with and cooperate with small *c* christians, but it is difficult for big *B* Buddhists and big *C* Christians to find common ground." Thay said this on the day he led the retreat for the staff of the International Fellowship of Reconciliation in Alkmaar in 1982.

"I take refuge in the Buddha," I said in a short letter to Thay, "and the Buddha takes refuge in Jesus." It was an example of small *c* christianity in dialogue with small *b* buddhism. In fact, for all the differences that a theologian or scholar might list, Christianity and Buddhism have much in common. "If Christians and Buddhists were living together in one house," Thay remarked, "it would not be stressful if compassion was at the center of their spiritual lives."

Small *c* christian that I am, I found Thay's form of Buddhism extremely helpful. Yet I never became a Buddhist, nor did Thay ever nudge me to become one. I never found the Buddha and Jesus interchangeable—never saw them as two men who, at different times and in different ways, achieved similar enlightenments and, as a consequence, illumine the world in comparable ways. Buddhism, as I experienced it in Thay's company, had many saints (bodhisattvas) who had a great deal in common with Christian saints, but I found in Buddhism no concept of God. Buddhism had many inspired sutras and other sacred texts but nothing that challenged and nourished me as much as the four Gospels. In Buddhism there were many helpful rituals but no Eucharist. The man we know as Buddha was the result of the sexual union of his royal parents. In the case of Jesus, his genesis was miraculous, God becoming flesh in the womb of the maiden Mary, a virgin. The historical Buddha died and his body was burned; Jesus died and rose from the dead. These are not minor differences, yet they never strained my relationship with Thay or reduced my gratitude for Buddhism. Thay helped me bring mindfulness into my life while making no effort to detach me from Christianity. His respect for Christianity was manifest. At one point he even sent one of his ordained monks, a former Christian, to live with Nancy and me—Thay had come to the realization that this particular monk, Gary, in order to continue on his way, had to return to Christianity. After a few weeks with us, Gary went from our house into the novitiate of a Trappist monastery.

The raft is not the shore

Among other small c christians who became Thay's good friends was Dan Berrigan, the American Jesuit priest and poet who had spent nearly two years in prison for burning draft records. Dan became one of Thay's visitors both in Paris and at Sweet Potatoes. "I was being healed," Dan wrote of those visits. "I was being healed of America, of the Western church, of the Jesuits, of the wounds of war, of prison, of the disease of making it, of my race in time against time."[17] One consequence of their time together was a book, *The Raft Is Not the Shore*,[18] containing the transcripts of some of their more formal conversations.

Dan Berrigan and Thich Nhat Hanh with Nico Tydeman, a Kosmos Center staff member, in Amsterdam

Their exchange began with the subject of memory and moved on to the Eucharist and death. As the days passed, they discussed religion in the world, life in exile, priesthood, imprisonment, self-immolation, economics, communities of resistance, and Jesus and the Buddha. Dan reached deeply into Christian sources, Nhat Hanh into sutras and other Buddhist writings, while both shared stories of decisive moments in their lives.

Memory, Dan ventured in their first taped dialogue, was a creative faculty that reunited—literally *re-membered*—a broken body, a broken soul. It re-membered not just what was and is but what could be. Thus a man like Martin Luther King could "remember" and describe, as he did in his "I Have a Dream" speech, a future without anyone in bondage. Dan's vision of what *could* be inspired two liberating questions: "How do we cease being slaves? How do we cease being slave masters?"

Thay was reminded of memory in another sense, as suggested by the French word *recueillement*—recollection—the attitude of someone trying to be himself, not to be fragmented: "One tries to become whole again." This was the beginning of awakening, of enlightenment, an event that can happen suddenly, in the blink of an eye. Nhat Hanh recalled the time he had meditated on the Christian Eucharist and suddenly understood the action of Jesus in identifying himself with bread and wine. With this act came "a drastic awakening"—the disciples of Jesus experienced enlightenment. They no longer lived in a phantom world.

Dan replied that the Eucharist, linked as it is to the last supper before Christ's arrest, brought to mind the death of Jesus. After the meal during which bread was broken and wine shared, Jesus experienced a blood-sweating agony in the garden of Gethsemane. Finally, having accepted his own death, he walked freely to his captors.

In each life, Dan said, every person has experiences that prepare him for death, as, for example, Dan's own close encounter with death while in prison. "Suddenly knowing I was dying," he told Thay, "was a very quiet and simple moment, and there was no fear."[19]

Thay suggested that Dan's close contact with death while in prison was due to his letting go of what he had earlier thought of as death and simultaneously his discovery that life and death are interconnected; one cannot exist apart from the other—they are as joined together as two sides of a coin. "That is why," said Thay, "when one has seen the real nature of things, he will acquire a kind of fearlessness—an attitude of calm—because he knows his death will bring no end to life . . . his existing does not depend on his 'being alive' now."

Thay's insight reminded Dan of his last visit with Thomas Merton not long before his death. In a talk with the novices about death, Merton spoke "with joy" as if anticipating his own. "He said the only thing that relieved the life of a monk from absolute absurdity was that his life was a joyful conquest of death . . . [the monk] was living apart from a world which paid death such tribute—racist, violent, militaristic—a kind of taxation exacted on people by death itself."[20]

Dan and Thay had both been educators, yet both agreed that classrooms are rarely the ideal environment for deep learning. One may earn a doctorate on a certain topic but fail to be transformed.[21] Dan recalled a distinguished seminary professor who traveled widely to give a lecture entitled "The Idea of Love in the New Testament." "I thought," said Dan, "that was a strange thing to talk about—the *idea* of love. . . . One reason for the deep trouble at the seminary was that there was no atmosphere around them inviting them to become Christians. Rather the atmosphere was inviting them to become experts on Christianity."[22]

The pirate and the child

Preparing for a lecture at the Kosmos Center in Amsterdam in 1982, Thay wrote one of his more important poems, "Call Me by My True Names." One of the treasures in our home is his gift to us of the poem's first draft, in which the original title is "call me by my own name." Here it is in its finished state:

> *Don't say that I will depart tomorrow —*
> *even today I am still arriving.*
>
> *Look deeply: every second I am arriving*
> *to be a bud on a Spring branch,*
> *to be a tiny bird, with still fragile wings,*
> *learning to sing in my new nest,*
> *to be a caterpillar in the heart of a flower,*
> *to be a jewel hiding itself in a stone.*

I still arrive, in order to laugh and cry,
to fear and to hope.
The rhythm of my heart is a birth and a death
of all that is alive.

I am a mayfly metamorphosing
on the surface of the river.
And I am the bird
that swoops down to swallow the mayfly.

I am a frog swimming happily
in the clear water of a pond.
And I am the grass-snake
that silently feeds itself on the frog.

I am the child in Uganda, all skin and bones,
my legs as thin as bamboo sticks.
And I am the arms merchant,
selling deadly weapons to Uganda.

I am the twelve-year-old girl,
refugee on a small boat,
who throws herself in the ocean
after being raped by a sea pirate.
And I am the pirate,
my heart not yet capable
of seeing and loving.

I am a member of the politburo,
with plenty of power in my hands.
And I am the man who has to pay
his "debt of blood" to my people
dying slowly in a forced-labor camp.

Vietnamese boat people

My joy is like Spring, so warm it makes
flowers bloom all over the Earth.
My pain is like a river of tears,
so vast it fills the four oceans.

Please call me by my true names,
so I can hear all my cries and laughter at once,
so I can see that my joy and pain are one.

Please call me by my true names,
so I can wake up

and the door of my heart
could be left open,
the door of compassion.

The genesis of the poem, Thay explained to his audience in Amsterdam, was linked to his efforts to rescue
"boat people" refugees adrift in the Gulf of Thailand in
1976–77. Using two rented ships, Thay, Phuong, and their
collaborators rescued eight hundred boat people. Many
others died at sea. One of these was a twelve-year-old Vietnamese girl who had been raped by a pirate and afterward
jumped into the sea and drowned herself.

"When I heard this story," Thay said, "my first response
was anger—anger at the pirate and others like him preying
on those who were fleeing from Vietnam. I hated them for
their deeds. But as I thought about the pirate who raped
the child, I realized I could not dissociate myself from
him. If I had been born in the pirate's village, if I had his
cultural and economic background, perhaps I would have
become like that pirate. In other circumstances, I was the
pirate. I was also the girl who drowned herself."

Thay asked his audience the question, "Who is the
enemy? Is it pirates? Is it Communists? Is it the Russians?
Americans? Is it political leaders? To answer the question
we must look closely to see where 'we' end and the person
we call an 'enemy' begins. We will find that the actual
roots of war are not human beings but intolerance, fanati-
cism, greed, hatred, and ignorance. These are the true enemies. We must encompass those we think of as enemies in
understanding and compassion. If we can begin dealing
with our inner enemies in an accepting and nonviolent
manner, seeing their dependent nature, we are truly making cause for a peaceful world. Our enemies are not man."

o caterpillar, in each point on your body I see + hell and paradise by the multitude,

for each measure you make with your body, you need the totality of time

the mendicant of Kapilavastu is still on the ~~Spirit Vulture Peak~~ Gridhrakuta Peak contemplating the splendor of this sunset

Sutami! what a surprise! ~~was~~ who said that the Utpala (blue lotus) blooms once in a million years?

The voice of the rising tide is heard by any ear that is ready to listen —

Call me by my own name
do not say that I shall depart tomorrow
because even today I still arrive.
look at me: when I arrive each second and each minute
to be a bud on the spring branch
to be a young bird, whose wings still tender, learning to sing on my new nest
to be a caterpillar in the heart of a flower
to be a jewel hiding itself in the heart of a stone in order
I still arrive, to cry and to laugh
to hope and to fear
my coming and my going are the breathing of all the sentient beings
the rythm of my birth as my death is the beating of the heart of all that are alive

I am the ephemera metamorphosing on the surface of the water
I am also the bird, who when the spring come,
fly to the river to eat the ephemera when it
just come out of its shell,
I am the frog swimming happily in the clear water of the pond
and also the grass-snake who silently moves around to feed
itself on the frog
I am the Uganda child, all my ribs are shown, my
legs are as tiny as bamboo stick,
I am also the person supplier of deadly weapons to the african & asian nations.

A page from first draft of Thich Nhat Hanh's poem "Call me by my True Name"

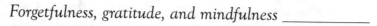

Forgetfulness, gratitude, and mindfulness _____

"Where does the outside world end," Thay asked, "and where do I begin? Our bodies reflect the outside world. The sun is our heart—we cannot live without the sun. The air is our breath and our lungs—we cannot live without breathing. The oceans and rivers are our blood—we cannot exist without water. Since we protect our bodies so carefully from injury, can we not see the Earth and all life as our body and protect it just as carefully? We have lost connection with the simplicity of our lives and move about in a state of confusion and forgetfulness."

The cure for forgetfulness is mindfulness, Thay often said. Again, recalling his experiences with boat people refugees, Thay saw how mindfulness can save lives:

"Sometimes the boat people encountered extremely dangerous storms—their boat could easily capsize. Yet in the midst of the storm if just one person remained mindful and calm, he or she could strongly influence the others. Thus, panic would often be prevented, and the boat would have a better chance of surviving the storm."

Being peace _____

Asked if he thought taking part in protest demonstrations was useful, Thay recalled how he and others practitioners of mindfulness had recently taken part in a rally against nuclear weapons in New York City, only the group he led walked very slowly. "It was a big demonstration—half a million people. Walking mindfully up Fifth Avenue, we carried a banner with the words 'Reverence for All Life.' Thousands of marchers passed by us, surprised, sometimes irritated, at our slowness. It took us five hours to complete the march that others walked in two hours. As we walked, I noticed that many pro-war and antiwar people, though they stood on opposing sides, often shared the same mind—angry, antagonistic, fearful, and dualistic. If we are demonstrating for peace, it helps if we ourselves are in a state of peace."

Many people in such demonstrations describe themselves as nonviolent, Thay noted, but said the label isn't accurate. "It doesn't help to see people as being either violent or nonviolent. Violence–nonviolence is a continuum along which people are either more or less violent. There are nonviolent people who are full of violent thoughts. There are violent people who are trying to become nonviolent. An army commander carrying out a military campaign might choose a strategy that tries to protect noncombatants, who uses a lower level of firepower than another commander. Even in war, one can be more or less violent in specific situations."

Peace activists, Thay pointed out, are often poor at finding ways to open channels of communication with those whose policies they seek to change. "Protesters write very good protest letters but are less able to write love letters. We need to write letters that the recipients won't throw into the waste basket."

Thay recalled a conversation with a demonstrator in New York who asked about anger and enmity. "When I think of President Ronald Reagan and his threats to use nuclear weapons," the questioner said, "I become very angry. I have to turn off the TV. I don't want to see his face or hear his voice." Thay responded, "We always deserve our government. Mr. Reagan is in yourself. He is because we are. This is because of that. This is not because that is not. Has our daily life nothing to do with our government? That is the question I invite you to mediate upon. Anger does not clear our minds. When anger occurs, recognize it; neither suppress it or give vent to it. Surround the person who has caused the anger with your compassion and understanding. You should be gentle with your anger. It is not different than yourself."

Peace is every breath—calligraphy by Thich Nhat Hanh

The supermarket as zendo _____

A question was raised about teaching mindfulness to children. "I propose that we turn our supermarkets into zendos," Thay remarked. "Many children are more eager to go to supermarkets than to zendos. Meditation halls are located not only at monasteries and Zen centers. A zendo can be wherever we practice mindfulness."

Thay recalled taking a group of children to a French supermarket to buy nails. The box of nails they found cost five francs, and the text on the box said the nails were made in the Philippines. "The nails were put in the box by children like you," Thay explained to the children, "who made only five francs for a whole day's work. The children were very happy to have work, but their pay was so meager that they were always hungry. These nails connect us—we are part of their hunger. How we live is connected to how they live. For a few minutes the supermarket was a zendo."

∾

Plum Village _____

In June 1984, a letter came from Thay inviting us to visit Plum Village, the community's new base since 1982. In August, driving an old Volkswagen we had at the time, we camped and picnicked our way from Alkmaar to the village of Thénac in the countryside northeast of Bordeaux. There we found the stone house in which Thay was living.

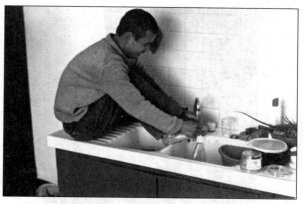

Thich Nhat Hanh washing his feet

It stood on a wooded hilltop to one side of an orchard heavy with ripening plums. A small, newly built dormitory became a temporary home for Nancy and me plus Cait and one-year-old Anne. Next to it was a larger guest dormitory.

By 1984, Plum Village was already becoming a center of pilgrimage and of teaching the basics of mindfulness. By incorporating several buildings a few kilometers away, called "the lower hamlet," Plum Village also had become a place of reception for Vietnamese refugees.

Life at Sweet Potatoes had been monastic in a minimally structured way but was becoming more structured at Plum Village. The schedule, whose borders were marked by the hammering of a board or the ringing of a bell, brought us together for meals, talks, work, sitting, and meditation.

The guests included Arnie Kotler and Therese Fitzgerald, who were in the process of founding Parallax Press, in effect a successor to the La Boi Press. Instead of homemade books printed in the tens and hundreds by Thay and Phuong, now, thanks to Parallax Press, their books

*Carole Melkonian hammering a
prayer board*

would be printed in the many thousands and efficiently
distributed.

At a table in the kitchen, Cait spent hours each day
with Phuong packing medications that were being sent to
addresses all over Vietnam. Such postwar aid was much
needed. Cait was enchanted by Phuong—the songs that she
sang and the stories she told. When they were together,
there was constant laughter.

Thay's room was just over the kitchen. One day Thay
asked me to bring him some papers from his desk, and,
in trying to find them, I noticed, amid the many letters,
envelopes with cash donations that friends had sent to
help with such projects as buying medicines to be sent to

Phuong and Cait packing medication; Andy Cooper to the left

Vietnam. "Thay," I told him, "there is a lot of money on your desk." He had been too busy with other things, he said. He asked me to gather the money together and pass it along to Phuong.

Arnie Kotler was bursting with energy. One day he decided to give the grease-encrusted stove a thorough cleaning. It was hard work. At a certain point Thay came to watch, after some time making the comment, "We never do that." Arnie abandoned scrubbing.

Processions

One of the things Thay was teaching those who made their way to Plum Village was his method of mindful walking.

Plum Village pilgrims; Nancy second from the left, Cait next to Thay

In the late afternoon each day he led everyone in a silent procession. The walk was prefaced with his advice that we practice slow, mindful breathing while at the same time being aware of each footstep, seeing each moment of contact between foot and earth as a prayer for peace. Our feet should kiss the earth, he reminded us. We went single file, moving slowly, deeply aware of the texture of the earth and grass, the scent of the air, the movement of leaves in the trees, the sound of insects and birds. As I walked I was reminded of the words of Jesus: "You must be like little children to enter the kingdom of heaven." Such mindful walking was a return to the wide-eyed alertness of childhood.

～

Sitting in circle in preparation for a procession

One will be three

As he tended to do with all children, Thay spent a lot of time with Anne. They clearly enjoyed each other's company. Sometimes his hand would rest for a moment on her head. Sometimes they sat silently side by side. He watched her playing with a plastic bucket and sand shovel.

His joy in children inspired this poem:

> *one will be three*
> *one will be ten*
> *we'll be back*
> *we'll be back*
> *on the ocean of Forms*
> *let us ride*
> *on beautiful waves*
> *to the mountains*
> *to the rocks*

Thich Nhat Hanh with Anne

the forests
and the humans' lands
off to the stream
out to the ocean
with the morning sunlight
on the wings of graceful seagulls
the snow, so white
listens to the singing
of a child.

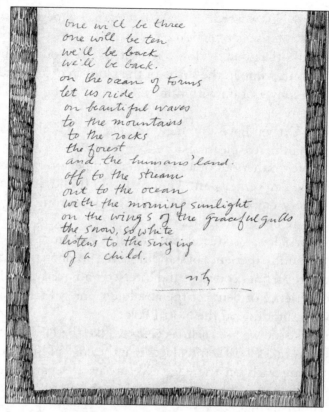

Journal page with the "one shall be three" poem

Everything is good

Since their time together in our kitchen making rice balls
a decade earlier, Thay had developed a deep affection for
Nancy. On one of the daily processions at Plum Village
she found him walking beside her, his footsteps replicat-

ing hers. Not a word was said but Nancy experienced a sense of intense connection.

On another day during our visit, Nancy found Thay sitting on a stone in the shade of the plum trees and had a helpful conversation with him:

Nancy: Do you have a moment to talk?

Nhat Hanh: Yes, please. Sit here on a stone.

N: I've felt rather out of it here. I'm not a person from one of the Zen centers, and I'm not an old friend, like Jim.

NH: (very emphatically) No, no! You are wrong. Maybe you are better than Jim!

N: When I was sixteen, standing at a bus stop, I had a profound experience of standing at the point on the globe where all lines converge and intersect—an overwhelming experience of being at the absolute Center. I felt as if I were standing on the North Pole.

NH: It's true we are each, as you say, like the North Pole. (Thay takes a stick and places it at the edge of his stone.) We are each on the edge. We are each separate, and each one of us has everyone within us.

N: How can that be?

NH: (Thay holds up a leaf.) As this leaf holds within it everything—all the sun, all water, all earth.

N: But it also makes you realize we do everything alone. Everything, every step—alone. Walk through life alone. Die alone.

NH: Yes. I told the people in the Zen centers in America, "Meditation is a personal matter!" (He smiles.) That means meditation is an exercise in being alone—in realizing what it is to be alone. There is a story in Zen Buddhism about a monk. His name was (pause) "The

Monk Who Was Alone." He did everything alone—ate alone, washed dishes alone—everything. They said to him, "Why do you do everything alone?" He said, "Because that is the way we are."

N: Lately, I've been reading so many things which all seem to pertain to my "North Pole" experience. I pick up a book or read an article, and it all connects. At first I thought it was a coincidence that so much of what I read is connected.

NH: (Smiles and shakes his head.) It's no coincidence.

N: I've read some of Merton. And about the Hasidic Jews. And the story of the Fall in the Bible—Adam and Eve. About how, before the Fall, Eve just stood in her place, and walked in the garden. God had given them everything they needed, and it was all good. Eve didn't know what evil was. Then when she was tempted to eat of the Tree of the Knowledge, of Good and Evil, she decided there wasn't enough for her, just standing there—even though she didn't have any idea what "evil" was. So by eating, she destroyed the garden. I've thought a lot about that here—walking slowly through the woods.

NH: But you know—good and evil are just concepts. Maybe even the serpent was good, and the apple. All good. It's like this stick. I can say, "This half is good, this half is evil." They're all concepts. Maybe Eve was even good after the Fall. You say "before the Fall—after the Fall." It's all the same.

N: The Hasidic Jews always are dancing. It's all holy, everything. But after Eve ate the apple, we don't know if she really was able to know good from evil—we only know she was ashamed. (Thay smiles.) Merton said Eve

Anne playing beneath plum tree at
Plum Village

wasn't good before the Fall and bad afterward. He said she was her True Self before the Fall and not her True Self afterward.

NH: And he also said, "Everything is good." (He smiles and stares at me)—and he said that in Bangkok (shortly before his death)! (Long pause.) You know, if you are really able to understand this, you can look at all the nuclear weapons and . . . (very long pause—Thay's eyes scan the distance) . . . and smile.

∾

Letting go _____

That summer stay at Plum Village was our last visit with Thay and his community. More and more people were coming to learn from Thay and, they hoped, to obtain face-to-face access to him. However, we noticed that our having one-on-one time with him excited envy from some of those who had not yet had the opportunity for more intimate guidance. By a fortunate providence, it had been my privilege to travel and live with Thay off and on for sixteen years when he was hardly known. Nancy had also gotten to know him both in our kitchen and at Plum Village. We realized we had had our turn. It was a perfect time to let go and create space for others.

I recall an important teaching moment with Thay in 1968, early in our friendship. We were sitting side by side at a conference being held at the headquarters of the Fellowship of Reconciliation in Nyack, New York. Thay reached for the journal in which I was taking notes, put it on his lap and drew a simple diagram on a blank page: four small circles arranged to form the corners of a square. Then he placed a fifth circle in the center. Next to each of the outer circles he wrote the names of four of my principal mentors: Dorothy Day, Thomas Merton, Dan Berrigan, and Al Hassler. Under the central circle he inscribed Jim Forest. Beneath the diagram Thay wrote: "Jim admires each of these people, but he is not any of the people he admires. Jim Forest is only a name. I is only a pronoun. Who is Jim Forest?"

This last sentence was, for me, a *koan*—a Zen question that cannot be easily answered. A *koan* feels like an arrow shot into one's back just out of reach of either hand. I knew instantly that this question was of life-and-death significance. I struggled with that question for a long time, in fact years, slowly coming to realize that I had long been trying to create a self that was a weaving together of my mentors, the people I most admired. One of them, of course, was Thich Nhat Hanh.

While I could easily have developed a worse method of shaping my identity, the best I could achieve from it was the construction of a strange disguise—a mentor mask. Whoever God had in mind in calling me into existence, it was not a mish-mash of others, however admirable, however inspiring. Finding mentors and learning from them was essential in the process of growing up, but finally I had to let go of my mentors and uncover my own true face.

Taking distance from Thay was along the lines of the proverb he had once shocked me with: "If you meet the Buddha, kill him." These few words are not an invitation to murder anyone but a summons not to make your life an imitation of someone else's, even if the other is Buddha himself, or Jesus. Even if you are a Christian, someone attempting to center your life on the person you recognize as God incarnate, you are not called to replicate Jesus in each detail of his life, insofar as it can be imagined, but to become someone new, someone who bears witness to his life and teaching, but doing so in a way that is as unique as your fingerprint. Each Christian, as I learned from Metropolitan Anthony Bloom, head of the Russian Orthodox Church in Britain, should become a unique but faithful translation of the Gospels—a lifelong project.

Letting go of Thay was a necessary step.

From time to time I re-read one of Thay's numerous books or listen to recordings of his lectures—many are available on the internet—and am filled with gratitude for the periods of my life that I either lived with him or was often in touch with him. Truly, I felt like a member of his community. This helped me, and in many ways still helps me, even though I don't often think about it consciously. Thay is just there. If I eat something mindfully, or walk mindfully, or spend a little time breathing mindfully, it is partly because my life has passed through his life. If I find my way into the present moment rather than wander into the ghost world of the past or the dream world of the future, I am partly being helped by Thay's example. If I breathe away anger and breathe in compassion or find a point of connection with someone I didn't want to be connected to, it is partly thanks to Thay's influence.

This book attempts to share some of the lessons I learned from Thich Nhat Hanh. I found it an obligation to tell these stories as a gift to others.

There is a lot to learn from Thay. Many would agree with me that he is one of the great teachers of the past hundred years. His voice will still be influencing people for many years to come.

But he is not the target, only an arrow pointing the way or, as Thay might put it, a finger pointing to the moon.

∽

Postscript

In 2005 the Vietnamese government gave permission for Thay to return for a visit during which he was allowed to teach and travel. Four of his books were issued in Vietnamese editions.

Thay returned for a second visit in 2007 and was warmly received.

In November 2014, Thay suffered a severe brain hemorrhage which resulted in his losing the ability to speak. He now communicates silently, using facial expressions, gestures, nodding and shaking his head in response to questions. He still has use of his left arm.

In October 2018, Thay (age ninety-two) returned to Vietnam to spend his remaining days there. His home is the Tu Hieu Temple in Hue, the same temple he had entered when he was sixteen.

Thich Nhat Hanh in a wheelchair surrounded by monks at Tu Hieu Temple

"Thay's health has been remarkably stable," reported a Plum Village representative. "When there's a break in the rains, he comes outside in his wheelchair to enjoy visiting the temple's ponds and shrines."

～

The present moment

When I first met Thay, he told me his personal name, given on the day of his ordination, was Nhat Hanh. It meant, he explained, "one action." Forty-six years later I think I know what that one action is. It is simply to live attentively in the present moment, awake to suffering, awake to joy.

Monk in meditation beneath a tall tree.
Drawing by Vo-Dinh

Appreciation

My thanks to Nancy Forest, Robert Ellsberg, Mobi Warren, John Williams, Fred Eppsteiner, Stephen Headley, and Tim Schilling for their part in bringing this small book together and making many helpful suggestions.

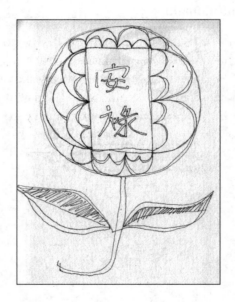

Notes

1. Founded in 1914, the Fellowship of Reconciliation is America's oldest and largest peace organization. Visit its website: https://forusa.org/.

2. The full text is in Thich Nhat Hanh, *Love in Action: Writings on Nonviolent Social Change* (Berkeley, CA: Parallax Press, 1993), 49–56.

3. At the end of his first tour, Nhat Hanh's first book in English, *Vietnam: Lotus in the Sea of Fire*, was published by Hill & Wang. It presented a history of the conflict and the peace proposals in greater detail. Thomas Merton wrote the book's foreword.

4. Thomas Merton, Recording #164.03, recorded May 29, 1966. From the Archives of the Thomas Merton Center, Bellarmine University, Louisville, Kentucky.

5. Full text of Dr. King's letter: https://plumvillage.org/letter-from-dr-martin-luther-king-jr-nominating-thich-nhat-hanh-for-the-nobel-peace-prize-in-1967/.

6. His host in that apartment, Stephen Headley, became my good friend. Steve and Nhat Hanh had lived together when Nhat Hanh was teaching at Columbia. Steve later became a Russian Orthodox priest, first in Paris and later in Vézelay, France. Thich Nhat Hanh relates various stories of living with him in *Fragrant Palm Leaves: Journals 1962–1966*, trans. Mobi Warren (Berkeley, CA: Parallax Press, 1998).

7. For a detailed account of the Phuong Boi period of Thich Nhat Hanh's life, see *Fragrant Palm Leaves.*

8. By 1964 the Buddhist hierarchy was more appreciative of Nhat Hanh's ideas. *Voice of the Rising Sun*, with Nhat Hanh as editor, was restarted and became one of South Vietnam's most widely circulated and popular publications.

9. The story of the draft-record burning and the trial and imprisonment that followed is told in detail in my memoir, *Writing Straight with Crooked Lines* (Maryknoll, NY: Orbis Books, 2020).

10. She is now Sister Chan Khong. She tells the story of her remarkable life in *Learning True Love* (Berkeley, CA: Parallax Press, 1993).

11. While the Hoa Binh Press edition of *The Path of Return Continues the Journey* is long out of print, the play is now a chapter in *Love in Action: Writings on Nonviolent Social Change* by Thich Nhat Hanh (Berkeley, CA: Parallax Press, 1993).

12. A *gatha* is a verse recited silently in rhythm with the breath as part of mindfulness practice.

13. The story of the postwar human rights debate is told in the chapter "To See or Not to See" in my autobiography, *Writing Straight with Crooked Lines*, 245–48.

14. The rule has since been published. See Thich Nhat Hanh, *Interbeing: Fourteen Guidelines for Engaged Buddhism*, 3rd rev. ed. (Berkeley, CA: Parallax Press, 1993).

15. Thomas Merton, *The Hidden Ground of Love* (New York: Farrar Straus & Giroux, 1985), 115.

16. Thomas Merton, *The Asian Journal of Thomas Merton*, ed. Naomi Burton et al. (New York: New Directions, 1975), 308.

17. Daniel Berrigan, *Ten Commandments for the Long Haul* (Nashville, TN: Abingdon, 1981), 28.

18. Dan Berrigan and Thich Nhat Hanh, *The Raft Is Not the Shore* (Boston: Beacon, 1975; reprint, Maryknoll, NY: Orbis Books, 2001).

19. Ibid., 5.

20. Ibid., 9.

21. Ibid., 23.

22. Ibid., 110–11.